GROW

The Field Guide to Personal Growth

Stories, Principles and Secrets
On the Journey of Personal Growth

Clay Staires

To my dad, the late Don Staires.
Dad, thank you for always telling me you were proud of me!
I was listening!

TABLE OF CONTENTS

GROW

The Ultimate Map to Your Personal Development

Clay Staires

Acknowledgments

I've been on the path for over 48 years and have never truly been alone. God, the Great Mapmaker, will always provide us with encouragers, teachers and supporters along the way. This is just one of His great benefits!

In the mid-nineties, I was in church when one of our pastors called me out and gave me a very encouraging message he felt was from God: "Clay Staires, your name is your destiny! You are moldable and teachable. God will use you to help people ascend to new levels of influence and impact in their lives." That man was Michael Sullivant and I want to thank him for hearing the voice of the God and being willing to share it with me. I've never forgotten that word, and it has comforted me in times of pain, hurt, and confusion.

I have also been blessed by having a tremendous family that has stood by me and encouraged me throughout my life. My mom and dad, Don and Shirley Staires, have been wonderful role models of servant leadership. My older brother, Mike, and two older sisters, Kelly and Sally, paved a smooth road ahead of me—thank you for providing me with a good last name that has opened many doors of opportunity.

Although it took me until I was 29 years old to begin listening, there have been several men who inspired and mentored me throughout my journey. Don Andreson, Mike Bickle, Jerald Freeman, Steve Youngblood, and Dave Jewitt have all been part of my "Fellowship of the Ring."

In 2009, I approached four men with an idea and a request. The idea was about me sharing my message and plan for personal growth with others around the globe. But before I could do that I needed financial support while I put it all together. Steve Mackey, Jeff Yinger, Ron Griffin, and the late Clark Milspaugh saw something in my story and in my passion that caused them to agree to join The Executive Circle. Thank you so much for investing in me!

And then there are my girls! Maddy and Clare, thank you for letting me be your daddy. You have taught me how to live with a father's heart for others. And, Lisa, my beautiful bride; thank you for believing in me and always loving me so well! "Blessed is the man who finds a good wife." I feel that blessing every day!

"Show me now your map." Elrond to Thorin in *The Hobbit*

INTRODUCTION:
WHY YOU SHOULD READ THIS BOOK!

It was dark and cramped, but it was the only place I felt safe.

I had just closed the door to the bedroom closet where I had run to find security. *Yes, here I'll be safe,* I thought. *Nothing can get to me in here.* No, there wasn't anyone after me. I had just reached the end of my rope—the bottom of my barrel. I was out of escapes!

Over the previous five years, all my emotional securities had been systematically pulled out from under me. I was 30 years old without a job, without any strong family connection, living out of a car (that had just been stolen, along with all my belongings), and preparing to walk through a very painful and ugly divorce that had already resulted in the loss of custody of my two-year-old daughter.

It felt like one of those scenes in a movie when the actor is up close to the camera and the background starts pulling away into the distance. I was falling… fast. The closet, with its darkness and small, confined space, was the only place that felt safe. Space, even the space of a small bedroom, was too open; too vulnerable. Without all my emotional and intellectual supports, I was left alone, feeling very exposed.

Here, I would be safe… for now.

It was the summer of 1994, the completion of a season of dismantling for me. You've heard the cliché, "Build on a sure foundation." I had been building my life for 25 years on a foundation of talent, ability, personality, skill and—wait for it… *entitlement!* It's not that I was wrong for doing that. It's just that growing up that way did not prepare me for, well, growing up.

I knew I had a purpose and a design for my life—and I also knew it was supposed to be different than what I was currently experiencing.

How is this happening to me?! I was the one destined to make it. I had all the external tools and resources needed to succeed: good grades, class president, great friends, influential family name, leadership positions, vision for the future, athletic ability and recognition, and tons of support.

Launching out from high school in 1982 was easy. My universe was so small, my thinking so limited, that I actually felt like I had already peaked in life. The rest would simply be "riding the wave!" However, there was this little voice in the back of my head that kept pinging out an alarm: *Are you sure you're prepared for what's coming?*

I just did what most of us do with that little annoying alarm—I shut it out!

I bring all this up because I'm sure I'm not the only one who does this. I've talked with hundreds of people over coffee, in my office, or on my porch who have been in this exact spot! Through tears (and a lot of nose-blowing), they are hit by something they weren't prepared for. What we've been doing has been working okay, so we just don't rock the boat. Just keep pluggin' away and hope for a break.

Can you relate to this?

Mike Tyson once said, "Everyone has a plan until they get hit." Boom! Wisdom from a guy who got hit—a lot!

Around this time, my dad received a book entitled *If It Ain't Broke, Break It* by Robert Kriegel. He had gotten it after going through his first open-heart surgery. Then, while still in the hospital, his physician and family friend informed him he also had diabetes *and cancer*! His life had unraveled fast, leaving him with a lot of questions.

I didn't want any part of that book! I wasn't interested in fixing anything—I wasn't interested in even looking hard enough to see if anything was broken! I was happy. Life was working for me. My eighteen-year-old philosophy of life was working, and would continue to work for a l—o—n—g time!

Or not.

This big, ugly monster that so many of us aren't quite prepared for is called *change*. For those of you who don't like the word "change," I'll use a kinder, gentler word: *grow*.

Growth will never come without change. We can so easily become creatures of habit—humans who get stuck in a rut and, rather than working hard to get out of it, work just as hard (or harder) to make the rut comfortable so we can stay there (and hope for the best)! Ahhh! Are you with me on this? Okay, you may not be able to relate, but you have a good friend who can, right? Good enough. We'll just say this is for "them"!

As I said before, I had built a foundation of talent and personality. My life experiences up to this point had taught me that I was awesome and that because of this inescapable fact, I was *entitled* to a smooth life! This overestimated sense of self shielded me from being able to receive instruction from others. Wonderful leaders and role models surrounded me but I always thought, *I know more than them and don't need anyone telling me what to do.*

If the word "punk" is coming to your mind about now, don't feel bad; you may be on to something!

I was the poster child for *growth without change*! It's a very popular group throughout the world, and our slogan is "Rewards Without Responsibilities!" Unfortunately, we keep losing members due to something called "reality," and the members we *do* have never attend the meetings because they don't have time for change! Something about being too busy! "But, please keep sending me the monthly rewards," they say. Ha!

In 1989, I got hit and found out I wasn't prepared for it. I would eventually come to discover it was just the first of a series of hits that caused my world to unravel and drove this larger-than-life personality into a four-by-four foot closet with the door closed tight and the lights turned off… just to feel safe. I didn't want to go out there. I was hurt and scared and just needed everything to stop while I caught up!

Now, I've used the word "change" a lot already, but let me take a moment and make sure we're on the same page with how we're going to define "change." This isn't just, "Hey Clay, we're going to change your shift at work. Can you come in an hour later?" No, the change I'm talking about is more like, "Hey Clay, we just had a meeting and we decided your position is no longer needed in the company. Please gather your things; your check's in the mail." *Big change!*

I often use the word "transition" for this type of change. "I'm in transition!" And transition *can be* a very good thing for us, because transition often leads to *transformation*. That is why I have come to embrace and lean in to change—because I love transformation!

I have a friend, Jerald Freeman, who has been pastoring a church for almost 25 years. He used to say, "We are all familiar with transition. We're either in the midst of it, just coming out of it, or heading into it." The question I want to ask is, "Are you prepared for it?"

If you're in the midst of a transition in your life, you need the understanding that's in this book to encourage you and help you navigate through the confusion and self-doubt that often accompanies these major "shifts" in our lives.

If you're just coming out of a transition, you need the lessons in this book to help you interpret your experience in a way that inspires you to live differently and to help others stuck in the prison of comfort or the valley of indecision.

If you're heading into a transition, you need the instructions in this book to help you prepare for what lies ahead so you can move through it successfully and confidently.

If you aren't in transition right now, you probably know someone who is and you may want to help them. You need the wisdom in this book to help your friend gain perspective on what is going on in their life.

This book is a map! Although each individual person may have different experiences and interpretations along their individual paths, the journey itself is fairly consistent from person to person. For instance, if you were traveling through Colorado from Grand Junction to Buena

Vista, you would probably choose to head east on Interstate 70 and then south on Highway 24. You would have some stops along the way to go to the bathroom or to get gas and some Funyuns, but you'd take the most direct route.

However, when I was 23 years old, I chose to hitchhike with an 82-year-old gentleman, in the middle of the night, in a pickup truck with no heat. He was a retired railroad worker who "knew all the back roads" and, much to my chagrin, kept referring to me as "boy." Yes, we made a stop along the way, but it was at his little house out in the middle of nowhere to pick up his dentures that I had to help him find! We eventually found them along the wall under his bed! I'm sure my "experience" was very different than yours, even though we left from the same place and headed for the same destination and made some stops along the way.

I'm glad you've chosen to pick up this book. You've taken the hardest step towards growth and personal development—the *first one*! Keep reading and don't quit! You're going to find a lot of stories, principles, and tools to equip you for success on your journey; this book is going to help you discover *your* map!

How to Read This Book

Growth isn't an event—it takes time! You need to be prepared for it. Personal growth is a lifestyle, but incorporating that lifestyle doesn't happen immediately. A healthy garden doesn't come about over a weekend, especially if it's had years and years of neglect and random planting.

18 months is a good initial timeline to consider. That's the real cost of personal growth. It's not just the price of a book or a seminar; it's the price of your time!

A significant part of the learning will be the *unlearning*! The process all begins with some measure of conflict between what you *thought* to be true in your mind and what you are *discovering* to be true in your experience. It's not that one has to be right and the other wrong; it's just that when there's a difference—and there's often a difference—it creates conflict. And it's at this point of conflict where you usually begin the process of learning.

The process of change can be a very intimidating challenge for most people, because change often includes an element of the unknown, and we often interpret the unknown as dangerous and scary. That's why we resist it. Even if my current circumstances are horrible, I can find myself choosing those horrible circumstances over the scary unknowns of "change," because they're familiar!

Chances are pretty good that, at some point, you're going to want to put this book down and stop reading. Why do I say that? Well, let's do the math…

> *this book is about change*
>
> +
>
> *most people tend to resist change*
>
> =
>
> *people may tend to resist the wisdom in this book*

I came to that point many times along my journey and I always had a very good reason (excuse) for why it would be better for me to stop. Be careful with this tendency.

There will be a sequence to each topic I introduce. First, I'll attempt to simply discuss the topic using some stories and experiences I've gone through, to see if you can relate to me in this topic. Do you understand? Are you with me? Am I the only one who has ever felt this way?

Second, I will go a little deeper into the topic to help educate on where it comes from and how it affects us in our daily lives. I hope you'll read this portion of each section and not only say, "Wow, I totally get where he's coming from", but also have some moments of saying, "Oh my, I never understood why I keep doing that. Now I get it."

And then finally, I hope to equip you with specific tools to help you move *away* from areas you have identified as negative and *toward* new positive ways of thinking, acting, and relating that bring joy and fulfillment to your life. Three goals for every chapter and topic:

1. Discuss to Relate
2. Explain to Educate
3. Equip to Grow

All of us are familiar with #1. We do it all the time at work, over the phone, with our friends, with our spouses and, sometimes, even into the air. We talk about things that are impacting our lives in an effort to discover, *Is there anyone out there who understands where I'm coming from?* This is very normal and healthy. We just want to know that we're not alone in dealing with our problems.

However, many times we'll want to talk about our problems, but we're really not looking for any kind of explanation or solution—we just like to talk about our problems. We all know someone like this, don't we? This can quickly degenerate into griping and complaining that, unfortunately, locks us into a pattern of resisting growth and change. Eventually, the only people who remain willing to listen to us are others gripers and complainers, and before long we can get stuck without realizing it. We've surrounded ourselves with other people like us, so we don't notice our negative bend or our resistance to growth—it looks so familiar and normal.

But #2 is a little trickier. Fewer people really care about actually discovering where their struggles come from and why they keep surfacing. It's very easy just to keep talking about them and blaming our struggles on the boss, our spouse, or the government than it is to truly dig in a little and sort through what is "my responsibility" in this thing. But for those who want to move forward, I'm sure you will learn a ton about where old, negative thought patterns and recurring negative actions come from. We'll talk about this in the next chapter.

At this point I would like for you to make a deal with me. I know you don't know me real well, but I'm going to ask for something from you, because I know it's going to come up and I know it will keep you from receiving the maximum benefits from this book. It's not a hard request. I just want to ask you to guard your mind from saying three words that will quickly shut the doors to growth and rob you of the treasures of wisdom that lie within these pages. So, here we go. Here are the three words I am asking you to guard yourself from thinking and saying:

"I KNOW THAT!"

These three words are responsible for the death and abortion of countless unrealized dreams and potential in people around the globe. We hear something and simply write it off with a flick of the head and a raised eyebrow as we say, "I know that." It's like an anesthetic that numbs us to new growth and change; it's the death knell for new revelation and enlightenment. "I know that" becomes our way of dismissing information that could really change our lives by rationalizing and devaluing its potential.

So, please accept my invitation to guard your mind from dismissing the depth of the growth potential in this book by saying "I know that." In fact, if you're willing, say it to yourself, out loud right now: "I will guard my mind from dismissing my potential for growth by saying 'I know that' as I read this book."

Boom! Thank you.

Goal #3 is the "Grand Poobah" of them all (yes, that was a Fred Flintstone reference!)! For those of you who are able to hang on and stay focused through the discussion and education of this book, to you will be the harvest of the equipping.

Yes, it's possible to just cut to the chase and go directly to the "how-to" part. Unfortunately, this is how many of us have been trained to respond to learning. "Just give me the answer!" And that will be enough for those of you who just want answers. But if you desire a new way of interpreting life that brings joy, peace and fulfillment, you will find that perseverance yields a valuable harvest of transformation. I applaud you and I salute you! Here's to the Journey!

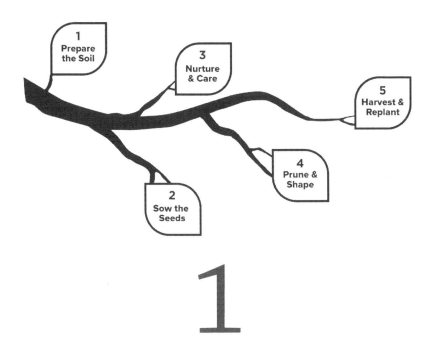

1

PREPARING FOR GROWTH

We've all heard the stories of how a great challenge has been thrust into a person's story without warning or preparation and how the shock caused them to feel like they were falling backwards into a dark hole. You may even have that story yourself. You know, the story that includes the words like, "I'm leaving you", or "We have to let you go", or "It's cancer". These are phrases that seem to redirect our life, in a hurry.

In Napoleon Hills' book, "The Lost Prosperity Secrets of Napoleon Hill", he refers to *the great unseen hand,* as the universal force that guides us and directs our external circumstances to form and shape us into the person we are intended to become. I've felt this hand in my life numerous times, but I can't say that I have always understood it's leading or recognized it's presence until it came crashing down on top of me. I guess "unseen" was the operative word for me!

In the summer of 1994, Travis Sewell and I were helping a close friend, Tommy Brown, move his family from Oklahoma to Washington State. I was hoping for a relaxing, scenic drive with my buddies out to the west coast. However, Tommy, the Army man who was moving to Washington to be stationed at the base in Tacoma, had envisioned a 50-hour non-stop death march. It was a painful trip on many levels.

My wife and I had been struggling for a few years but we had been working through it with the help of friends and some marriage counseling. I was thinking we were doing OK. While on the trip, I had called her a few times to stay in touch but was never able to reach her. Now at this point of the story, YOU can tell something's coming can't you! But, unfortunately, I didn't see the freight train that was just around the corner headed my way. Even though there were so many blaring signs along the way, I didn't see them ("unseen" was, again, the operative word). When I finally reached her on the phone, there were a lot of "words" exchanged but that was pretty normal for us. But then she dropped the bomb – "Clay, I've moved out and I've taken our daughter."

BOOM! A mental and emotional IED had just gone off at my feet. I was falling.

Napoleon's "hand" felt like it had just pushed me over a cliff!

"I wanted to be the one controlling my life! I knew what was best for me!"

This way of thinking left me without any resource to interpret my new reality.

Obviously I was NOT in control. I was working so hard to keep things going the way they had been going. I was holding on way too tight to things in my life that were never meant to sustain me. I didn't understand correctly how "growth" occurred in a person's life. I had no grid for the process of growth. *I didn't understand "the hand"!* As a result, I interpreted its activity in my life as cruel and unfair. I didn't know how to GROW appropriately, so "the hand" had come to prune! Wow, even now that sounds so ominous and unsettling. But I'll talk about pruning on down the path in Chapter Five.

(You can check out Appendix C for the conclusion of this story.)

WHAT AM I PREPARING FOR?

Keep in mind that growth isn't just a black-and-white formula that moves everyone from point A to point B; growth is a process that occurs as you add or exchange new learning for old preconceived ideas. This book is entitled *Grow* but it could just as easily be called *Change*. But who's gonna buy *that* book?

People resist or avoid change for many reasons; habits, values, beliefs, comforts, fears—the list goes on and on. But growth will never occur until you become willing to change. And sometimes circumstances have to get pretty desperate for us to "get willing."

My journey through "the valley" took about thirteen years! As with Job in the Bible, everything was returned to me seven-fold. However, it first had to be taken away. It wasn't taken away because I was being punished or because I had done something "wrong," it was removed simply because it was in the way of my forward progress. Does that make sense?

This is why so many times people emerge from a season of struggle very happy that it happened—because of what they have learned. They may not ever want it to happen again, but they are happy it happened. It was through my "call to the wilderness" that I learned the pace of life and the way of change. It's also where I acquired the tools and resources to, not only survive the quest, but help others navigate through their wilderness of change as well. I call it the wilderness because it feels so lonely and desolate.

Today, there are many, many people in that wilderness—moving forward with no real plan or map. You may know some of them, intimately. If you're like me, you can work hard to make the wilderness a "dwelling place." But that's not the plan! The wilderness is always something to pass through.

Unfortunately, not many people make it to the other side successfully, and even fewer people who, after making it out, turn around and head back in to help those still stuck! But that's the big picture thinking in all of this! The *process* in the wilderness will facilitate and nurture personal change. However, the *purpose* of the wilderness is so that, once you have walked out, you become willing to reach back and encourage those behind you! The apple tree doesn't live off of its own fruit—the fruit is always used to feed others. We'll get to more of this later.

WHY DO I NEED TO PREPARE FOR GROWTH?

Preparation is key! I played football in high school and had a lot of success at my small school (I went on to play at the University of Oklahoma for Barry Switzer, which is a great story, but outside the context of this book). The point is: I knew how to play the game. So it seemed only natural that, since I'd had success as a player, I could have as much success when I became an assistant coach.

Unfortunately for me—and for the Memorial High School football team where I first coached—knowing how to play and knowing how to coach are two different things! This is another example of how something as simple as a little success can blind us from the need to *grow*!

When I was playing ball, I just did what came naturally, and it worked! If someone came to tackle me, I could just run around them or outrun them to the end zone. Boom! Problem solved!

However, when it came to helping someone else do the same thing, I was pretty clueless. I wasn't prepared. I didn't ever learn the game; I just learned how to *play* the game. And because I had some success playing the game, I interpreted that as "knowing the game" and being able to teach it to others.

The MHS Chargers went 0-10 the season I was an assistant coach.

Obviously, I didn't know what I thought I knew!

It's the same way with our personal growth: preparation is key! Trying to prepare when you're in the midst of some forced change in marriage, job, kids, health, school, relationships, etc., can be very, very difficult. In fact, because of lack of preparedness, most people never get through it. Instead, they get stuck in a dead zone of drudgery and just hope that things may change someday, if they could just get a break.

Are you relating to any of this? If you are, say out loud, "Yes, this makes sense." I know it may sound a little hokey, but trust me—it's critical in helping you prepare your mind for change. Mental changes must be *voice-activated*! If this is making sense, *say it out loud*!

In the First Phase of Growth, called Preparation, we are going to walk through the Four Steps Of Preparing For Growth. Just like preparing a garden or an orchard before planting, it is imperative that we prepare our minds and spirits for the new thoughts and ideas that will be introduced to us as we grow.

We will then dive in to the Second Phase—Sowing—where I'll introduce you to some new thinking about where and how growth begins, some ancient wisdom on personal growth that will leave you wondering, *Why didn't anyone ever tell me this?* These new ideas and ways of interpreting life will be like seeds you sow into your prepared mind and spirit. Your preparation will allow these seeds to find a welcoming place to be planted. Without preparation, your old mindsets and conditioned thinking can be a very hostile place for new ideas.

In the third phase of this book, we'll tackle the tough questions of how to ensure that these new ideas stick and grow. I'm sure you're very familiar with learning something new and thinking, *This is awesome! This will change everything!* only to find it becoming a distant memory after a couple of weeks. That's classic! Did you know that our old conditioned mindsets are hardwired for self-preservation? Our conditioned minds are constantly guarding against a foreign invasion of new ideas that would help move us forward. That's why so few people actually break through and find success and fulfillment in life.

The work of personal development starts out with learning new thoughts and activities that can easily offend our old conditioned minds. And before you know it, we've found all kinds of excuses *not* to start exercising today, or eating healthy, or looking for a new job, or… you fill it in! That awesome new idea was sown onto the hard, fallow soil of your conditioned mind; it never had a chance to take root. Bingo! The old mindset can check "mission accomplished" on its to-do list: "Keeping You From Challenging Your Thinking."

How often has this happened to you? How many new ideas have you started with, only to find it lost and forgotten three months later? I'm confident that this Third Phase on Watering will challenge you and encourage you at the same time. It's not rocket science; it's mainly about being deliberate and consistent!

This will take us to the Fourth Phase: Pruning! Hey, now that sounds fun doesn't it? Well, although it may not sound like an enjoyable process for the plant, it's vital to its overall health and *growth*. Without pruning, the life-giving nutrients and resources needed to keep the plant healthy and vibrant can be diverted across too much surface area. Trying to keep everything going becomes an overwhelming task and the plant uses all its energy just to keep up the *status quo*. Flowers can't bloom because resources are being rerouted to keep the leaves alive so the whole family can keep going and I can get all the bills paid and I can feel successful and finally prove to my Dad… oh, wait! I was talking about plants, wasn't I? Oops!

We'll finish the process with the Fifth Phase: Harvesting. How do we know when we're ready and the process is over? What is the fruit? How will I know if it's ripe? How do I collect the fruit, and what do I do with it? This may sound like a lot of questions but the great thing is that they are all *questions of a harvester*! And that's where you're headed! You are on a course towards becoming a harvester of fulfillment, wisdom, joy, peace, hope, resources, time, talents, happiness, and on and on and on! This is what you were made for! Once you have a harvester's mindset, you'll wonder how you have lived so long without it!

However, it's hard to be a harvester when you haven't yet learned the sower's mindset, and you can't develop a sower's mindset until you lose the survivor's mindset that plagues most everyone on the planet! Growth is a sequence and a process. When we haven't yet learned how to sow, the thought of harvesting can easily seem overwhelming and out of reach. Even though you work really hard at achieving personal success, it will always seem to be just beyond your grasp.

I have made it through more than one of these wildernesses of change! I've learned the ancient path and I want to share it with you. To learn the path will require a willingness from you to be open to new thinking and ideas. Not everyone who enters the wilderness makes it out on the other side. Some, get stuck in the valley of indecision and go around and around in circles. One pivotal truth I've learned about this process: you don't have to know the path yourself. you just want to make sure you're following someone who has a map!

This book is that map. If you will closely follow the advice and processes I present here, you will learn the map and be able to navigate for yourself, as well as for others. If you will be willing to let go of some of your old conditioned mindset and embrace some new paradigms, you will no longer be resistant to change and the fears it can bring. If you will stick with it and do the work, you'll emerge on the far side of the wilderness triumphant, and your ultimate victory will come when you turn around to face the valley and head back down the path to help others!

Everyone wants the rewards of growth, but not all are willing to embrace the responsibility required to attain them. Will you be the person that's willing? You *can* do this! You've already taken the first step by reading this far!

Don't stop now!

Keep moving forward! Keep growing!

DECIDING TO GROW

Just because you *want* to grow, doesn't mean that you *will*—at least not consistently in the desired direction. Any type of positive, effective growth has to be *intentional*. It's a deliberate activity that must be set as a priority in the midst of the noise of life—and if you're like me, you've discovered that life can be *very* noisy! Schedules, commitments, requirements, meetings, family, kids, expectations, relationships, Facebook—let's face it; there are a ton of things violently fighting for your time!

Yes, it's true that growth happens constantly in nature, but when was the last time you saw someone's lawn that they didn't maintain or walk into a flower garden that never got any attention? It doesn't take long before things get out of hand and chaotic. It's the same way with our lives. Healthy, fruitful lives require *intentionality*.

I have spent many years being a mentor to 18- to 26-year-olds. Many of them have come to me over the years with an excitement for personal growth and development.

"Clay, will you be my mentor?" they ask.

I will almost always begin with giving them a small task to complete and then ask them to contact me once they are done.

About one in four call me back within an acceptable time.

The *idea* of growth was really cool for them. But the *doing* of growth was a whole different ballgame because they didn't understand the concept of *intentionality*. They were just kind of waiting for it to happen because they wanted it to.

Deciding to grow personally is very much like deciding to go to college. Making the decision doesn't mean you automatically pass your classes. (If you're like me when I was 19, this may come as a shock to you! "Dad, is a 1.8 GPA good?") I guess you could say you have to make the decision every day, *intentionally*.

Like many other endeavors, decisions require follow-through, so let's talk about a few things that often get in the way of that. Let's avoid the obvious ones like being lazy and unmotivated, or the classic "I don't need to change" attitude, and talk about some reasons that usually end up surprising people…

UNEXPECTED OBSTACLE #1: NOT CREATING SPACE IN YOUR LIFE FOR CHANGE

Are you crazy-busy? Man, I know a lot of people who are! This isn't necessarily a bad thing; it's just that, if we're not careful, we can get so busy that we don't see how anything else could fit into our already packed lives. I have had many conversations with people who are interested in expanding their capacity relationally, emotionally, spiritually or even professionally, but who just don't have time. They're moving so fast that the new stuff they haven't been doing just gets thrown on to the pile of "good things I don't have time to add to my life right now." They see the new ideas and paradigms of change as *extra* things to do and they just don't fit. This is because they have a paradigm that tells them they can simply add "change" to their day like they can pick up a gallon of milk on the way home from work.

Because we don't fully understand the implications or the requirements needed for change, we can easily go to the workshop, read the book, hire the coach, listen to the lessons over and over… and still never move forward. This is because change is much more than just an *add-on*. Remember talking about transition and transformation earlier? This type of change requires *replacement* thinking, not *add-on* thinking. Something has to *leave* before something new can *come in and stay*. Notice I said come in *and stay*. It's easy enough to read something good in a book or hear some good insight on the radio, but if I don't do any replacement thinking, then the chances of that new information sticking with me are very slim.

Have you ever found this happening to you? You hear something you think is really insightful and try to make a mental note to include that thought in your life. But ten minutes later, you can't even remember it as you attempt to explain your newfound wisdom to a friend! I hate that! It's often simply because there's no space for the new information to fit.

The need to create space in your life for change usually comes as a surprise to people when they come to me wondering why it's not working. Replacement takes time. Old habits, values, and attitudes don't just go away when we hear something new. Old thought patterns have to be broken! That takes time and a lot of intentionality.

UNEXPECTED OBSTACLE #2: THE TIMING IS OFF

This often comes up when we try to force change upon someone—even ourselves—when there is already some kind of mental, emotional, educational, or relational pressure going on. We all have our limits and need to be aware of them. Getting married and having children while you're still trying to go to college full-time and hold down a job is very difficult. Trying to add some intense personal development to all that is a bad idea!

I've encountered this very scenario before, and we determined that their personal development should not be an add-on but simply a scheduled, intentional time each week to talk about, "Wow, how are you doing with what you already have going on? Do you have any questions? Has your spouse threatened your life yet?" We'll get to more of this when we address the issue of balance in our lives.

Often, when the timing is off because of some other major pressure, we will try to rush things and our primary goal becomes to discover the "what and who" of the problem rather than the "why and how." The "what and who" can be discovered pretty quickly without a lot of reflection and need for change. It's like your math teacher just giving you the answer rather than walking you through the process and teaching you how to arrive at the answer (I hated that!). This works for a time, but eventually, we have to learn the process and not just memorize the answers. This is connected to Obstacle #1—we need to take the time to dig in and discover "why" we have come to specific conclusions and "how" we need to respond so we can move forward.

I've always liked the expression, "Give a man a fish and he'll eat today; teach a man to fish and he'll eat for a lifetime." That's great—unless you have a man dying of starvation in front of you. The timing to teach is off. Feed him first, then teach him to become a fisherman when he is fed and ready.

UNEXPECTED OBSTACLE #3: YOU DON'T HAVE THE RESOURCES OR TOOLS NEEDED FOR SUCCESSFUL GROWTH

Americans will spend over $11 billion this year in self-improvement products. Bookstores are filled with rows and rows of books and resources promising the help you need. But when I say that you don't have the resources you need, I'm not talking about a book or a seminar—I'm talking about lacking an internal receiver to make growth happen.

We are extremely blessed with information! But that's not the real problem. More information isn't the complete answer. The resources we lack are those that help us with interpretation and application! We like what we're reading and hearing, we just don't fully know how to interpret it for ourselves and apply it to our daily lives. We don't know how to rightly incorporate the new information into our existing value system. At best, we hit up against Unexpected Obstacle #1, trying to add the new information to an already crowded life.

No, the resources we lack are mental, emotional, educational, spiritual and relational:

Mental Resources—Our minds are so packed with data from our information-crazed world that we simply lack the bandwidth to process new ways of thinking. A total crash becomes the only thing that brings us to a point where we realize we need to change. But if we're not careful, we'll simply start over again with the same filters and add-on thinking. It's a tragic cycle that many, if not most, people are experiencing in their lives, robbing them of the joy, peace, and fulfillment they long for.

Our brains are wired to think what we've always thought, and new information is either deemed as "agreeable" or "disagreeable." The tragic outcome with this is that we get new information important for growth, but it doesn't go beyond that first filter. We may quickly "agree" with some new information, but that "agreement" lacks the ability to change us before we're on to the next thing.

Or, even more tragic, we may "disagree" because it doesn't align with our current paradigm and just toss it out before even taking time to consider it. Our busy minds, constantly on the prowl for what's new, lack the capacity for change. We have a desire for change and even a momentum for it, but then—*squirrel!*—we get distracted by any sudden movements.

Emotional Resources—According to researcher George Barna, "Adults essentially carry out the beliefs they embraced when they were young." Barna's research has shown that "a person's lifelong behaviors and views are generally developed when they are young—particularly **before** they reach the teenage years. A person's moral foundations are generally in place by the time they reach **age nine**. Fundamental perspectives on truth, integrity, meaning, justice, morality, and ethics are formed quite early in life." In essence, the researcher noted, "what you believe by the time you are 13 is what you will die believing." *What?*

Someone in your life taught your habits, values, and belief systems to you. Either directly or indirectly, the way you think is a product of someone else's influence. Somewhere along the way you adopted your habits, values, and belief systems as your own and determined that they would become the truth upon which you would govern your life. From that point on, you began to build your life upon these determined truths.

The problem is that no one teaches us what to do when these established truths are challenged by life circumstances that occur while sharing this planet with seven billion other humans.

I have been a Life Coach for many years and have discovered that, with most of the people I've coached, the primary issue comes from trying to apply adolescent foundations to their adult life circumstances. As a result of this conflict, they get angry and start blaming and pointing fingers and yelling and manipulating and threatening and talking bad about the other person and wanting to fight and… hmmm… does that sound adolescent to you?

It's not that we're bad for doing this; it's just that we have reached the limits of our emotional resources to deal with our life circumstances, so we tend to freak out a little. The success I've enjoyed with my Life Coaching clients has simply come from helping them expand their emotional capacity enough to be able to interpret their current circumstances differently.

Adult situations require an adult emotional capacity to solve problems. The great difficulty comes in letting go of the old ways of thinking we feel have been so right for so long. It's almost like we have to accept the fact that mom and dad were wrong (or, even more painful, *right*) all along! This can be especially hard when the person I've trusted for so long was *me*! *Could I have been wrong?* We'll talk more about this later in another chapter.

Educational Resources —Most of us have never really learned *how* to learn. I've been a consultant, mentor, and trainer for years now. Before that I was a high-school science teacher for 15 years, and before *that,*, I spent 17 years in the public educational system as a student. I have spent the lion's share of my days on this planet either teaching or being taught. This experience has brought about some painful revelations, one of the most painful being this: *most people don't know how to learn*!

True learning must begin with a *pursuit* of information—a question! But, although I would contend that the United States has the best educational system on the globe, the majority of our classroom learning doesn't come from inquiry-based *questions*. Rather, most of our classroom instruction is focused on information-based *answers*! We move kids from class to class; they turn in homework they copied out of the book (or from their friend ten minutes ago); the teacher talks; the kids take notes (maybe); the teacher finishes and asks for questions and…

Nothing.

We have been trained *not* to ask questions. When I was a science teacher, I once had a student tell me he didn't want to ask questions because he didn't want me to know he didn't know the answer! He actually said that! Then he followed it up with, "I didn't want to look stupid." The very essence of a student is that they ask questions! But we have lost that sense of inquiry and imagination in our educational system. The pressures to "teach to the test" have caused teachers to plow through textbooks of 500 pages and that weigh 15 pounds! Lecture is king! Those who can memorize are prodigies! Although they are out there, teachers and schools that have maintained the emphasis on discovery and asking questions are very rare.

I was the same way when I was in school, though. I really only had three questions for any of my teachers: "When's the test?" "What's on the test?" "Is there any extra credit?" I never learned how to *learn*. I learned how to *memorize*, but that only worked if the question was straight off the memorization; if I had to use any measure of critical thinking, I was in trouble.

Does this sound familiar? I know this experience isn't true for everyone, but it's true for a lot of people—maybe even you! Our capacity to learn is simply limited, and as a result, we don't know how to change the way we interpret and apply new information. So we just keep on doing what we've always done and hope for the best.

Spiritual Resources —This resource provides an anchor for us as we encounter the stormy waters of daily circumstances. Where are you finding your anchor? There are a number of verses in the Bible that describe God as being unchanging, the same, eternal, One that has always been and always will be. That sounds like a pretty good anchor!

However, I often want to use my own personality, skills, or talents as my anchor. I've also heard of people (never me, of course) using their jobs, their money, and/or their possessions as their anchor.

Choosing unreliable anchors like those truly sends us into a downward spiral in the midst of life's struggles and pain—it's what sent me to the closet at the beginning of this book. I had chosen my anchors poorly.

Even as we do our very best to keep from capsizing, without an anchor, we feel like life is totally out of control and without purpose; we begin to slip into an emotion that was never meant for human beings: despair! It's so easy, when under pressure, to disconnect from the omniscient, omnipresent, all-powerful, never-changing, passionate Lover, and Friend who becomes an anchor that allows me to weather any storm. God is the only One who knows my *true* design! To turn to any other source is vanity, and chasing after the wind.

Relational Resources —This one is really painful! Given what I've already said about our limited capacity mentally, emotionally, and educationally, it's a wonder any of us are able to get along with others for any length of time! How we do relationships is strongly influenced by what has been modeled to us. The girl who says, "I want to be just like my mom," is just as influenced as the girl who says, "I'll never be like my mom." It's just in opposite directions.

My wife and I do quite a bit of pre-marital counseling with all the twentysomethings we mentor each year, and this conversation works its way to the surface in almost every single session. We relate to others according to the way we have been shown to relate. Even if we don't like what we've been shown, unless we intentionally and diligently learn a new pattern, guess who's gonna grow up just like daddy? We'll talk more about this when we discuss "Clearing The Weeds" in the next chapter.

How Does Growth Happen?

Growth is always happening. When asked this question once, I replied, "We're all in the process of becoming someone. The real question is, 'Are you becoming who you want to become'?" I thought that sounded pretty good, until one of my mentors, Dave Jewitt, responded with, "Clay, it's not just about you becoming who *you want* to become. It's about you becoming who you were *designed* to become". Okay, he wins! That is a much better way to phrase the answer! Thanks, Dave!

And that's what the rest of this book is all about: growing into your design! Becoming who you were created to be! As children, we're often asked, "So, what do you want to be when you grow up?" It's cute when you're eight, but when you're 18, that question can be very scary.

Many kids at this age lack a sense of real, personal identity, which causes them to answer along the lines of what they want to *do* rather than who they want to *be*.

Unfortunately, many people jump onto a life path based upon what is easiest, or what they think will be the most fun, or what they think will get them the most money or success. None of these reasons are inherently wrong; they just dismiss any consideration of pursuing the path they have been destined to pursue.

And it's producing some disappointing results. Mercer Consulting Firm research shows that half of U.S. employees are unhappy with their jobs! This gives us a hint that what we're doing isn't working real well. Do we need more proof to confirm we will continue to do what we've always known to do until what we've always known to do leads us to a place where we don't know what to do? (read it slowly and it will make sense!)

Remember that research by George Barna? "What you believe by the time you are 13 is what you will die believing." Did you take the time as you transitioned out of adolescence and into adulthood to dive into the conclusions about life you developed? Did you pause to see if what you believed when you were young would serve you well in adulthood? No one does that! We just assume it's worked so far, so it must be "the way it is." And off we go into our twenties holding on to a reality we developed when we were ten, eleven, or twelve years old.

This is not a good idea.

Even if we had great role models and a wonderful childhood, the simple fact that our brain was still a long way from being developed should alert us that we may have come to some shaky conclusions. But, unfortunately, we press on, and by the time we're thirty, we start sensing something's not right, we hang on, and we wait for something to change and make life better. But little happens (maybe kids are in the picture now and distract us from the underlying issues) and our thirties are filled with the hope that hard work and endurance will pay off in the end.

By the time we reach our mid-forties, we're worn out. Our fifties can cause us to go inward, gut it out, and wait for retirement to escape the rut we feel we're in. Or, many times in our fifties we come to the conclusion that we just can't do it any longer! The significance we've been waiting on hasn't arrived or hasn't been as fulfilling as we had hoped. We can feel like we've wasted so much time waiting for something that never arrived.

In our sixties we can focus more on self and our retirement when we can do what we've always wanted to do. Unfortunately for those who have worked their entire lives to reach the final goal of retiring, depression and a sense of uselessness often can be found in the pot at the end of the rainbow. And how bout those that are in their sixties that encounter the reality that retirement and slowing down isn't an option? "What, I can't get off this desperation train?" Wow, that can lead to all kinds of negative outcomes that ultimately destroy our hope for the future, which, if we're not careful, will lead us to entertaining some very dangerous thoughts. Discouraged desperation over a long period of time will always lead to depression and death.

Does this make sense to you? Can you see yourself somewhere along this timeline? I was smack in the middle of it! Thankfully, I got a jolt at thirty years old, and it awakened me to the need for growth. Up until that point, I didn't really feel there was a need for me to grow personally. I was okay—it was everyone else who needed help! I was just waiting for my "break".

If this is making sense to you, say it out loud: "This is making sense to me."

The principles laid out in this book are taken from nature. I use the metaphor of planting and nurturing seeds in a garden until they have grown and matured and produced fruit. I don't mean for this to be cheesy; it's truly quite profound if we allow ourselves to be simple and uncomplicated for a while. These principles have been born out of my own life story as well as the stories of hundreds of people I have had the privilege to mentor and coach.

We're going to walk through a system I've used with hundreds of people: The Five Steps To Successful Personal Growth. Each step comes with a tool to help you evaluate where you are and how you can begin moving forward with your positive personal growth. If you will stick with it and do the work necessary, these steps will lead you to the freedom that, to this point in your life, you may have felt was only available to a select few people but never for you!

Chet Holmes used the term "pigheaded determination" in his book *The Ultimate Sales Machine* to express the level of energy you will need to maintain during your growth. I tend to use the word "intentional" or "deliberate." Without this attitude, growth will turn "wild" on you and weeds will overtake your garden in a hurry.

This system I relate in this book is a great way to visualize your progress. It's not a formula to help you avoid struggles. In fact, the steps are designed to take you directly into the very fire that will purify the way you interpret your circumstances, setting you free to live the life you have been designed to live.

Here is a short outline of the steps using the metaphor of sowing seeds in a garden.

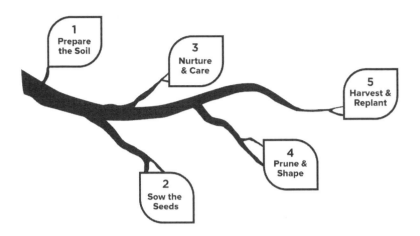

In this picture, you are the gardener and the seeds are your thoughts and interpretations of your circumstances. Most people don't take the time to tend their garden very well, so they get what they get and just hope for the best. In this book you'll learn the skills and mentality of a *master gardener*!

Once you have discovered your *identity*, you can begin to understand your life *purpose*.

Your purpose will help give your life *direction*.

Your direction will help determine your *actions*.

And your actions will help lead to your *production*!

This is what true life really is: *life filled with purpose and production*!

However: the movement is not up to *us*; we don't control how quickly we grow or how much we grow! You see, movement is a fruit and fruit is a product of a healthy plant. No master gardener sets their sights on just producing good fruit and then neglects the process. They know that the "process is the thing" – if they prepare the soil, plant good seeds and provide what is needed, good fruit will be a product of their labor. To attack this from the other direction is fatal. If we just try to produce great fruit without considering the process, at best, all we can hope for is a temporary harvest.

This kills people who want control! A control mentality says "I know what I need," or, "I know what's best for me," or, "It's my life, let me decide".

THE PROGRESSION OF DEVELOPMENT

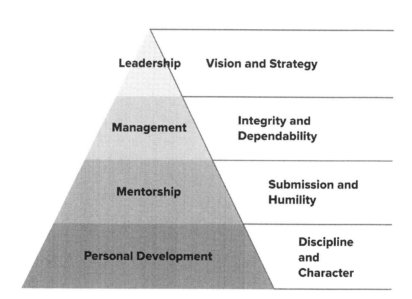

All growth is based on the foundation of personal character and discipline. Without these two qualities, growth can become corrupted and arrogant.

How do we grow? What does personal growth look like to you?

When you think of moving forward, what does that look like to you?

Is it vertical movement? Horizontal?

A ladder? A staircase? Some kind of continuum?

Take a moment to get a mental picture of what "moving forward" looks like to you.

I once got a picture of my heart being made up of many different "pools," where I was looking at my heart from above, and each of those pools was filled with water. I interpreted this picture as a great confirmation that my heart was full and even overflowing. It felt wonderful, as I patted myself on my back. But then the mental picture began to shift to a side view and I could see that, while each of the pools was full, not all of them were the same depth. Immediately I was humbled. Over time, however, I realized the meaning of the picture. Our heart can be in many different maturity levels all at the same time. We are not just one big mass moving forward and backward in maturity—some areas can be growing and expanding while others remain stationary.

I have come to describe the process of growth as not being a linear movement, but looking more like concentric circles, a new concept that truly changed my life—and the lives of hundreds of people that I have coached and mentored over the years. I am growing out and expanding!

Does this look familiar?
It's how growth happens in
nature!

I may be struggling in one area of my life, but that doesn't mean I'm stuck completely! It's very possible that *other* areas are growing even

21

though one isn't. It's possible for one area of growth in my life to be hindered while the rest may continue to grow really well. To understand growth in this manner is to be free from the disappointment of feeling like you have gone back to square one when something "bad" happens.

Have you ever had that feeling? Have you ever felt like you're gaining ground in your life, then something happens and you think, *I thought I had already learned that lesson!* Not only is this frustrating, but it can easily lead to hopelessness and eventually a sense of failure. The end product to this way of thinking is to quit. Most do! If you fail enough times, you'll eventually quit.

This is why it's so important to think about your growth in the correct way. How you think growth will happen is very important to this process. If you're not careful, you may experience successful growth, but because it doesn't *look* like what you were expecting, you can misinterpret it and think you're not growing at all.

One very important concept to remember throughout your journey: *It's possible to be in more than one place at a time!* You are not one big clump moving from point to point, where good days bring good, forward movement and bad days bring negative, backward movement. I'm sure you've encountered this back and forth feeling and gotten very frustrated, as if you aren't gaining much ground.

Bruce Springsteen sang a song back in the late '80s entitled, "One Step Up And Two Steps Back." Man, I can relate to this! Can you? If you can, *say it… out loud*: "Yes, I can relate to this!"

A THOUGHT TO CONTEMPLATE...

How much of your thinking was developed through a personal mentor who sat with you and helped you interpret your life experiences through a lens different from your own? As opposed to… How much of your thinking was just picked up along the way as you did the best you could to interpret your life experiences through the lens of your own limitations and prejudices? You can only think what you think! It's impossible for you to think anything other than what you think without some influence from an outside source. You are limited to "your thinking". That's why we find ourselves staring at the ceiling at night trying to figure things out only to find ourselves going around and around in circles always coming to the same conclusions! *"Ah! I can't figure this out. But I should be able to figure it out, but I can't... but I should... but I can't….".* It drives me crazy and keeps me from being able to fall asleep. We'll talk more about this later.

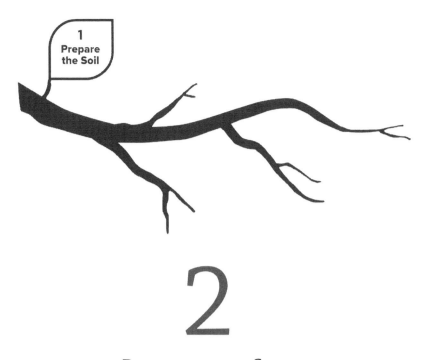

2

Prepare the Soil

Break Up The Ground

Lisa, my wife of 15 wonderful years, and I have spent many of our years together training young college-age leaders and helping them navigate through the very confusing waters of their early twenties. It's so wonderful to watch as they encounter "reality" for some of the first times in their lives without the buffer of their parents. There are few things in life more gratifying for us than playing a role in the development of another person!

Martha was the very first young leader that accepted our invitation to come live with us and spend a season of her life in intentional personal development. She had just graduated from college and felt she had a window of time so she accepted our invitation. She stayed for two years! We lived at Shepherd's Fold Ranch - a summer camp in Avant,

Oklahoma. Martha lived by herself in a 17' X 70' mobile home about a quarter of a mile away from our home. She worked at the camp during the summer as our Camp Director and then did several odd jobs throughout the year to make ends meet. Can you imagine being 22 years old and choosing to be isolated in Avant, Oklahoma (population 300!)? She was willing to embrace the difficult process of getting prepared for growth. She allowed "the soil" of her heart, mind and spirit to be prepared for a lifetime of healthy growth.

Martha had many hard nights as she wrestled with loneliness and isolation. We spent many nights holding her while she cried and encouraging her when she was confused. She watched her friends get married and start their careers. She had so many questions about why all these "magical things" weren't happening for her. Her jobs had her doing menial tasks that few others would stoop to do. She became an expert at plunging toilets and "shoving the balloon down the crap pipe" to open up the sewer lines to the septic tank. She even learned how to use the tractor and hay spike to put out round bales for the horses in the winter.

First things first - you see; a deliberate choice to grow in character and discipline *before* you attempt to grow in position and wealth will always be a decision to follow the road less traveled. But she was willing to wait and be patient! Her two years in the "greenhouse" prepared her to head to Law School in Washington, D.C. where she now practices law.

Obviously, everyone doesn't require a mobile home out in the middle of nowhere and a "crap pipe" (sewer line) to have success in his or her personal growth. But Martha's example of the willingness to "prepare the soil" became the standard we used with many others that followed in her footsteps. Her journey became the model we have invited others to embrace. And today, many years later, we have had hundreds say, "Yes" to the Process of Preparation.

How 'bout you? Would you be willing to say, "Yes" to the preparation? Without a "yes" in your heart and mind at this point, the rest of this book won't make much sense to you and may even become offensive.

Growth is a progression. With each page you turn, there will be an invitation to embrace the process. Yesterday's commitments will not be enough to sustain you in today's challenges. The enthusiasm you felt in Chapter One will not be enough to support you as you walk through the fires of Chapter Five. You will need to actively engage in the process.

For those of you that are willing, lets "turn the page" and keep going. If you're unsure, it's OK to put the book down while you go and consider the cost of your growth. A very wise man once said, "No man starts to build a house without first considering the cost". This is a wise saying worthy of your time and consideration.

The value of breaking up the ground before we start planting new seeds in a garden is clear enough without going into a sophomore biology lesson. But let me say that, when I meditate on the metaphor of hard, fallow ground it becomes quite alarming. Unyielding, packed soil in my life is simply a result of me shifting into "routine mode," where I'm stuck in a never-ending daily cycle of moving through A then B then C, then waking up and starting all over. It's not just my daily schedule; it's also the way I relate to my spouse or my kids or my job. It also creeps into the ways I spend my time and resources. I just get stuck.

This routine, although good for systems management, can suck the life right out of life, creating a shell around our hearts and minds that shields us from entertaining thoughts outside our boxes or comfort zones. You know what I'm talking about! We gradually organize our life and get it to a point where it's all in place. Because somewhere down the line *that* became a priority for us—to get to a place where everything was calm and predictable. And finally we get there. You've got the right job—making the right paycheck—that provides the right house in the right neighborhood with the right car in the garage... you know where I'm going here.

At the foundation of this type of thinking is a sense of settling as opposed to continuing to move forward. We just get to a certain place and... stay. We see this at work when we say things like, "I don't have the right job, *but it will do,*" or "It's not the right paycheck, *but it will do.*" Life isn't really going the way you want, but you just conclude *this will do.* The *this-will-do* blanket of familiarity covers us up and lulls us into a mindset of complacency.

Your life was never meant to be diminished or reduced down to a routine! Yes, routines can help us manage better, but "managing your life" isn't the ultimate goal! LIVING YOUR LIFE is the goal!

Sam was a successful businessman who owned a company he had run for fifteen years. The company had grown in size and in stature in the city. Expansions were made regularly, and new staff was added as well as new ventures within the scope of the company. Sam held significant positions of leadership in the local Chamber of Commerce, Rotary and on the Economic Development Committee assigned by the Town Council. Sam was a leader in his business and in the community.

But behind the scenes, Sam's marriage was struggling and had been for many years. The marriage was a classic picture of codependency, but he didn't see it. His duty as the husband was to protect and emotionally support his wife. This was what love looked like to him—he needed that "job" for his own sense of well-being.

Sam's wife, on the other hand, had numerous issues of self-confidence and relational dysfunctions. She needed her "job" of feeling victimized and rescued by her husband for her sense of well-being; she expressed her love by letting him be the knight in shining armor he loved to be. They were a perfect dysfunctional match! And they had been this way for twenty years. (By the way: please understand that these roles can easily be reversed as well. The husband is not always the rescuer!)

Sam and his wife each had their own important role to play in this dysfunctional relationship. Although it was draining both of them and the pressure, just under the surface, was building and building, they thought this was how you love someone. Even though marriage was difficult, they just hung in there and waited for something to change their circumstances and make everything fine. Well, that "something" finally happened, but it wasn't what they were expecting.

Sam decided he was finished. He felt he could no longer do it, and besides that, he no longer *wanted* to do it! Out of exasperation and desperation, one day in the midst of yet another argument, he let his wife know he was done. "I'm through! I'm not going to do this anymore. I'm outta here!"

Now, just so you know, the "Sam" in this scenario is a conglomeration of many different men I have coached and had coffee with over the years. "SAM" is an acronym for "Same As Me," because it's also a very good description of the path *I* was on back in my twenties. After so many years of holding on to the conclusions that had been put in place while he was in junior high, Sam realized they didn't work anymore.

It could be very easy to look at Sam and say, under your breath, "Duh!" But don't be too quick to judge this lack of understanding. Instead, use Sam's story to begin taking inventory of the conclusions *you* are holding on to. I'm sure they're not all bad. Some are probably very healthy and appropriate. However, are there some that linger, maybe in the back of your mind, that keep you prisoner to repeated habits you wish you could get free from? Old patterns of dealing with stress, relating to people, feelings about your self, or the ways you respond to pressure?

So, we need to do some internal inspection of our lives and break up the hard soil of our routines? Below is a short little tool I use to try and get a bigger picture of where a client may be when they start this journey. Take a moment to use it; evaluate your current circumstances. I got the idea for this from a friend of mine in Edmond, Oklahoma. He is a part of a medical group that has started a clinic that embraces the health of the whole person.

Remember, it's just a tool. It's not an accusation or a reality that's set in stone. If you don't like the results, over time you can change them! That's what this book is all about!

THE FOUR WHEELS OF HEALTH

"It's more important to know what sort of a person has a disease than to know what sort of a disease a person has." Hippocrates

On a scale from 0-7, 0 being very low and 7 very high, rate yourself on how you think you're doing in each of the Four Wheels Of Health. Then connect the dots in a circular fashion. Compare "your circle" to the "complete circle". This exercise is to help you become aware of weak areas in your "Health Profile".

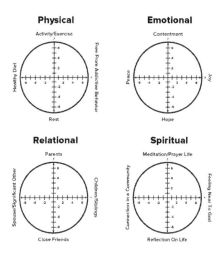

Any surprises? Anything you didn't see before? Or were your weak points already very familiar to you? How long do you want to stay stuck in your routine? Would you like to break up the hard soil that keeps you from growing and moving forward? If you would, say "Yes"… out loud!

TAKE OUT THE STONES

To move forward, we often have to let go of things that are holding us back.

As I said before, growth isn't rocket science—it's a very natural thing for all living things. However, for reasons we don't always understand, we can easily resist this natural process of growth and movement. We reconcile this resistance in our minds by creating a logical reason for it to be there—we become masters at inventing *excuses*. Whether it's blame or procrastination, if we're not careful, we'll always have a logical reason (at least to us) to *not* move forward.

These excuses act like rocks in a garden that keep new seeds from finding a place to take root. We have a desire to grow, to lose weight, to exercise, to stop smoking, to learn that new skill… but we never really get there. Somewhere along the path between desire and destiny, we get distracted and derailed.

I'd like to submit to you that the real tragedy isn't getting derailed—it's blaming it on something other than ourselves: "It's not my fault," "They're not hiring," "I don't know how to," "That's not fair." And as a result, we lose any traction for growth because it's always out of our control.

Excuses always leave us as the victim.

This reminds me of one young lady my wife and I spent quite a lot of time with, a wonderful girl we have truly enjoyed knowing. She was always so appreciative of everything she was learning. A few years back, she was finishing her last semester in college and discovered she was still one class shy of her requirements for graduation. Her first response was "That's not fair"—a very common, yet unproductive, way of dealing with disappointment.

After talking with her for a while, we came up with a plan to talk with the dean of her department about using her "work experience" as an independent study to get the credits she needed for her degree.

Surprisingly, the dean agreed—all my friend would have to do is fill out some paperwork and pay the fees, which were minimal in the grand scheme of things.

So, the plan was made and I forgot about it. A few months later, I asked her how it had gone and she told me she hadn't gotten to it yet. "What?" I replied. "Why not?" And that's when they began coming up: *excuses*. "I haven't had time," or, "I don't have the money right now," or, "I'm not sure what to do," and my personal favorite, "I'm waiting for them to call me back."

These excuses were simply her rationalizing her decision to *not* grow! At the same time, they were wreaking havoc with her self-esteem because they always made her feel out of control and victimized. Excuses become tools we use to reconcile our decision not to take responsibility and just blame our problems on our circumstances.

You must confront these excuses that hold you back and eliminate them from your emotional first aid kit. They aren't helping you!

The poor thinking which supports these excuses creates your conditioned mindset that often resists change or new ideas.

You've heard the cliché, "Insanity is doing something the same way over and over and expecting a different result." Well, it's the conditioned mindset that causes us to keep doing the same thing and hoping for a different outcome. I've done that a lot—just waiting and hoping that somehow I would get a break and things would change. I used to be the director of a non-profit organization where I battled hard with this mindset. We were always out of money, and I would blame it on low donations or low attendance or the need for more employees who could help. Although these may have been a reality, I made the mistake of letting those obstacles *create* the reality rather than navigating through them witcreative thinking and taking the responsibility of leadership that had been given to me. Because I kept blaming rather than taking responsibility, the problems never got solved! Can you relate? If you can, say it out loud: "I can relate to this." (even an audible whisper will do).

This is why all personal development is based on the foundation of discipline and character. These two qualities are vital to taking personal responsibility for your life.

How would you answer this question: *Can you live within boundaries and get along with others?*

Before you answer, consider these follow up questions: How much of your time is spent frustrated about having to remain within the rules? What does your house, car, desk, or apartment look like? What kind of order is in your day? Have you ever considered yourself to be a procrastinator? Have you ever felt like your personal relationships or your job performance have been negatively influenced by your inability to follow through?

You may not like the boundaries, but have you learned to stay within them?

With which phrase do you best identify? (Circle one of the following phrases)

"I Change my boundaries to fit my lifestyle"
OR
"I Change my lifestyle to fit my boundaries"

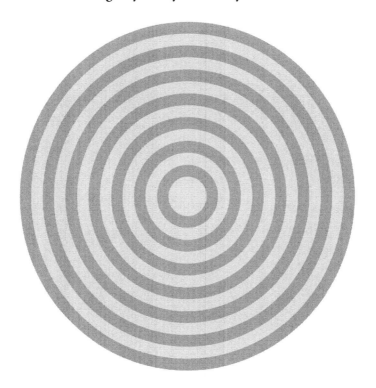

Take a look at the above picture in regards to boundaries. Let's say the inner circle is the original boundary. I made it small, not because it *is* small but because it *feels* small. There is a tendency to want to push the boundaries and see what I can get away with. This is called "rejecting discipline," though you may know it better by the misinterpreted term *"personal freedom!"*

If I do get away with it, I take it as permission and now I think, *It's okay for me to do this.* Then when someone calls me on it, I tend to get upset with them rather than realize it's about me. Have you ever done this?

If left unchecked, I'll continue to expand these boundaries to include whatever I want until I'm so far out from the original boundary that it seems impossible, even silly, to return. I write off the original boundary as irrelevant and therefore not necessary to obey. I have moved the boundary to fit my lifestyle! Not good!

The inner circle represents the personal discipline and character needed for personal growth. By constantly rejecting discipline and character, we gradually widen the circle of acceptable behavior and thinking, expanding the boundaries to include what we want. until we are so far away from discipline and character that it seems impossible to return. We have redefined 'reality' to mean something totally different than what it was originally.

> *I have redefined my reality to include whatever I want!*
> *Truth becomes what I say it is!*

So where does it stop?

Do you feel like this is something worth looking into? Can you see where a lack of discipline can have a huge effect on how you think?

Would you be willing to make daily, personal decisions that will keep your lifestyle within the boundaries? This is called **discipline:** rules governing conduct or activity.

Would you be willing to maintain discipline in the midst of discomfort? This takes **character**: personal qualities that are supported by consistent action.

Are you aware of specific excuses you've used over time to put off your personal growth? I'm sure you're like me in that you have a pretty good idea of the reasoning behind your procrastination. It's very important to identify these excuses so you'll quickly recognize them for what they are instead of allowing them to influence you.

You may also be very aware of some areas in your life where you have been pushing back the boundaries for a long time, warping your reality. Areas you know are inappropriate (or at least you thought that at one time) but have been rationalizing for so long that now they seem acceptable and even enlightened.

Take a short minute to write down what's coming to your mind in these two areas. Don't put it off until later—later rarely ever comes. Just go ahead and take two minutes and do it now. Writing them down doesn't mean you have to change all of them by next week—it just helps you engage in the future process of clearing them out.

For now, just write down what you already know to be true. This is an important part of *deciding to grow*. Decisions require actions!

MY STONES

Excuses I tend to use to rationalize my resistance to change are:

Areas where I know I have pushed back the boundaries so I could do what I wanted rather than stay within the rules are:

If you took a moment to write some things down, congratulations! You should celebrate! You are on the journey and are making progress! Great job!

Writing things down means you are intentionally engaging in the growth process! Now be careful not to fall into the trap of thinking success only comes when you complete the journey. This is a dangerous way to think; it will always leave you feeling frustrated and impatient. Embrace the journey!

CLEAR OUT THE WEEDS

Just so you know, this blaming mentality will eventually turn against you and attack your self-worth. It would always happen to me. I'd start by blaming external circumstances, and then, if I didn't change my course, my thoughts would eventually attack me and run rampant in my mind: *this is hard; I don't know how to do this; I'm not a good leader; I'll never be able to be a successful leader.* Over and over this would happen!

It's important to understand that none of us start our gardens from scratch. No, they've been growing for as long as we've been alive, whether we've been deliberate or not. So before we can have any hope for healthy growth and fruit in our garden, it's vital that we address the issue of weeds and other "wild growth" that have taken place over the years.

Those weeds outgrow and overshadow the growth you desire in your garden, stealing valuable nutrients away from the good plants you intended to grow. Some weeds even produce chemicals that attack surrounding plants to eliminate any competition. Left unchecked, weeds will take over—you'll never be able to produce the garden of your dreams. Your negative thinking will do the very same with your life!

One of my favorite scenes in *Braveheart* is when Uncle Argyle and young William Wallace are at the funeral of William's father (you know, the "outlawed tunes on outlawed pipes" scene). I love the comment Argyle makes when he notices William eying his sword. He knows what the boy is thinking, and he doesn't disagree with it, but he also knows there's a proper sequence. He turns to William and says, "First learn to use *this* (as he taps him on the forehead), then I'll teach you how to use *this* (as he raises the sword)." Argyle knew that if William simply ran with the sword, without learning how to think correctly, he would never see his fifteenth birthday. How you think is the most important thing about you!

I have mentored hundreds of people through the years. They often envision themselves listening and learning as we spend time together, thinking that just hearing new ideas solves their problems. What always comes as a shock to them is how much they actually need to *un*learn in order for those new ideas to fit. In most cases, it isn't about learning some new information or skill—it's about becoming aware of the old mindset blocking the new thinking from taking root. Even though we feel like we've heard the answer to our problem, it quickly slips through our fingers as we fall back into the ruts of our old thinking. We need to weed our gardens.

This old, negative thinking was what kept the young gal from being able to move forward and get her degree. There's more to that story… we sat down and began to talk about what was holding her back; through tears she began to express how afraid she was to graduate. Her fears had caused her to devalue the need for a degree, especially the one she would be receiving. "Everything I want to do, I can do without a degree," she said, in an attempt to convince herself she didn't need to do anything.

Here was this wonderful, intelligent young lady who was very capable of getting a position in her field—but totally paralyzed by fear. Our discussion continued and it wasn't long before we discovered the root of her fear: her self-esteem was very low and she was petrified at the thought of interviewing for jobs and being rejected. A degree meant she would have to enter the marketplace with all its competition. The idea of being chosen over someone else was outside her box—she didn't feel qualified and couldn't see herself as a success. As a result, consciously or unconsciously, she backtracked and figured out a way to keep that uncomfortable situation from happening. She had even gone through the graduation ceremony, but when it came time to finish, her conditioned mind imprisoned her in the fear of rejection and failure.

Around that same time, she attempted to take some accreditation tests she needed to complete her certification, and the same fears strangled her. Passing the tests became *bigger* than Mt. Everest… insurmountable! "I'm not smart enough," she said one day in my office. As you may have concluded, she didn't pass the test, so she devalued her degree even more. "A degree's no good without the certifications, and I can't pass the test."

So time moved on. I would occasionally ask how the process was going, but unfortunately, that deep root of fear continued to produce the same fruit of inaction.

Can you relate to my friend? I know I can! *How* you think is the most important thing about you! Poor mindsets can really hold us back from experiencing the growth and success we desire.

Here's a quick little equation to explain how our interpretations (thinking) influence our actions.

$$A \quad + \quad B \quad = \quad C$$

A = Your Situation
B = Your Interpretation
C = Your Action

C is always related to B, not A! In other words, your actions are always determined by your *interpretation*, not your *situation*!

Most people focus on their situation and circumstances and never can quite get their actions to change. It always depends on something that's usually out of their control: "I'm waiting for (A) to change!" That's the beauty of the stuck mindset: change always depends on something else, and usually that something else is out of our control.

Brilliant!

People get trapped waiting to win the lottery, waiting for the right roll of the dice, or waiting for someone else to do something so they can succeed. People wait for their boss to give them a raise or for their spouse to love them better or for the stock market to go back up before they change the way they think! This is poor thinking and it will continue to produce the same result—poor actions. And here we are again, feeling like we're going crazy, because we're expecting a different result even though we keep doing the same thing over and over!

Another way to say this is TFBAR! Okay, maybe it makes a better acronym than an actual word, but it's very true. Follow me here:
Your Thoughts will always dictate your Feelings,
which will always shape your Beliefs,
which always determine your Actions,
which always produce your Results!
TFBAR!

Thoughts ® Feelings ® Beliefs ® Actions ® Results

If you aren't getting the results you want, you have to start with adjusting your thinking. You must remove all the stones (excuses) from your garden so the new healthy seeds can take root. It's what's on the inside that determines the outside. To focus only on working harder to change your actions is, at best, temporary and, at worst, causing you to shut down and close off your feelings and act in opposition to your beliefs—which is not very healthy.

MY WEEDS

Are there areas in your life where you know you have some wrong thinking? Any areas where you have been waiting for the situation or circumstances to change before you decide to do anything about it? If you can think of these areas, continue to engage in the growth process by writing them down.

It's not uncommon for the weeds of inappropriate thinking to go unnoticed and undetected. It may be hard for you to answer the question, "Where are you thinking wrongly?" It's interesting how easy it is to not see the nose on your face. If this is the case for you, you may need to get some advice from someone to help you identify these weeds.

One hint in detecting weeds—they grow fast (promising quick emotional relief) and don't produce usable fruit (in fact, sometimes they produce *poison* fruit). Inappropriate thinking is often revealed by thoughts that lead to quick anger and mean words that get out of our mouths before we take the time to think about what damage they may cause. I call these episodes "weed flashes," and they occur often in parents at little league sport events.

ADD IN THE FERTILIZER!

Natural fertilizer is all the "crap" that's happened in your life! All the hurt and pain, the bad decisions, the big mistakes, the deep wounds, and the unexplained losses. It's the stuff that stinks, the stuff that we don't want to talk about, the stuff that burns our eyes when we get too close to it... the stuff that kills us if we spend too much time around it.

Fertilizer is an important ingredient in natural growth. The rotting, stinking, decomposing material we used to value for a different reason now becomes very valuable to the growth of the seeds in your garden. The cast-off garbage that once sat in the center of your dinner plate but now sits on top of the compost heap in some out-of-the-way location in the backyard, far from view of any respectable company. This is the fertilizer in your life and it's time to put it to good use!

Most people lock these bad memories away behind thick emotional walls and vow never to open the door for anyone, for any reason. We convince ourselves that if we never open the door, what's behind it will never be able to hurt us again, and we'll never have to think about it again. Well, you know that's not true, right? The junk we attempt to lock up always has a way of breaking out. So, we try harder to lock it up. We expend too much energy shoving it back, deep into the dark, and then have to be on constant guard to make sure it doesn't get out so nobody ever finds out about it.

It's exhausting!

All it takes is one small misstep and out it comes with a vengeance! All that pain and all that hurt is unleashed on someone else—or maybe even on yourself.

It's time to settle the issue of that locked door, because behind it is a treasure, hidden underneath all the confusion of the pain, hurt, and disillusionment. We'll get to this more in Chapter 4 when we cover how to process the "crap" in our lives so it can actually become a powerful tool to aid in our growth and the growth of others.

PUT UP THE BOUNDARIES

This past year, I have been surveying all my audiences when I have been fortunate enough to travel and speak. This helps me gain a better understanding of who is sitting out there and what life issues are currently causing pressure in their lives. When given the chance to rate their primary stressors, 82% of the people I surveyed indicated that one of their top three sources of pressure and stress was a lack of balance in life. For whatever reason, they feel there are some areas getting all the attention while others are sacrificed or neglected.

Most often, after further inquiry, this survey revealed that the things they *want* to do are what get sacrificed so they can fit in all the things they *have* to do. Wow, that's no fun! And, over time, it drains our emotional, mental, and physical reserves to the point where we are convinced we just need a few days' rest; just a little bit of time to do something else.

In other words, to get in balance, we often feel we have to stop doing one thing so we can start doing something else. The problem is that most of us don't feel like we *can* stop—at least not until the summer when we take our vacation. But that's a trap, too! Because once we get back from our vacation, we realize how much work has backed up. So immediately, all the benefit of the relaxing vacation is sucked away as we jump right back into work mode with a vengeance. Ah! How do we fix this tug of war?

What if I told you that it was possible to be in two places at the same time? This might confirm your opinion that I'm loony! Well: *it is possible to be in two places at the same time*! It's what I call being "in balance."

Here's how it works. Most people look at life through a singular lens (their personal perspective) and see most decisions as an "either/or" option. I have to choose one or the other; to have both is rarely possible. And even if it is, it usually comes with the stipulation of a compromise, so rather than getting 100% of either one, you have to be okay with 50% of both. This is limited thinking, and it will almost always result in feeling that one thing will have to be sacrificed to gain another.

Did you see the Coke Zero "And" ad campaign? In it, a guy gets hired for a job then looks at the recruiter and says, "And?" He ends up getting stock options! This is the type of mindset that understands it's actually possible to be in two places at one time.

Let's look at it this way: when we're feeling out of balance, some type of external force pressing in on us is often the cause. That one force, or multiple forces, can be so strong that we feel closed-off and isolated until that's all we can think about. We have no choice! It must be this way! Our answer to the problem quickly becomes—stop the external forces!

Although that's what our junior high conclusions would like us to believe, that can't be the only way. That would mean everyone would have to quit their jobs, stop paying their bills, and never talk to their in-laws! No, balance is not about eliminating external forces—it's about creating *internal* forces to counteract the pressure. We must have *push back* in our lives! Every time I have felt overwhelmed and out of balance, it has been a result of my lack of push back. I don't mean you actually say no to your boss, your teacher, or your spouse the next time you feel they have added some pressure to your life. No, what I'm talking about is having boundaries in your life. The way to have internal push back is to simply determine what type of impact you want to have on the earth.

If you're not careful, all your time can be eaten up with doing things that have no (or very little) intrinsic value to you. Yes, going to work and making money is nice, but having that as your ultimate destiny in life will lead you down a lonely road.

I get this! By the time we get home from work, we're tired and just want to veg out! I've even had the experience of getting so caught up in the lives of people on a TV show that I forget to think about my own life! Maybe that was the point of watching the show to begin with. Now *that's* out of balance!!

You must identify some activities of intrinsic value to you, then add them to your life on a consistent basis! These activities will provide the internal push back we need to achieve balance. Is it playing an instrument or exercising? Spending quality time with friends and family? Being outdoors and taking on physical challenges? Serving others through your church or community organization? I guarantee you there are multiple activities you enjoy that bring intrinsic value to your life, providing push back and bringing balance. If you feel you don't have any space for these activities, then I would suggest that either you lack healthy boundaries or you just don't realize where that space can be created.

A new Nielsen report says the average American over the age of two years old spends more than 34 hours a week watching live television—plus another three to six hours watching time-shifted programs on their DVRs.

Wow! Up to 40 hours a week watching TV? Maybe we could start here when we're looking for some time to carve out?

Last year, *Scientific American* featured an article by Christie Nicholson, who writes, "Objectively time is constant. A minute is a minute. But when we have a lot to do, it usually feels like we have less time. Now a study finds an interesting wrinkle in time: when we busy ourselves with *selfless* tasks, time seems to expand. In [an] experiment one group of subjects were given a period of free time to do whatever they wanted, while another group had to do something for someone else. Those who did something selflessly perceived themselves as having more time than those with no obligations. Those subjects also reported a stronger sense of personal power and effectiveness."

You must find space in your life to push back and give, both to yourself and to others.

Below, I've listed many categories of hobbies and activities people engage in to add value to their lives. This list is far from exhaustive—if you don't see a category, just add it at the bottom. Take a couple of minutes to identify as many activities as you would like in the categories that interest you. This will be the beginning of your push back arsenal!

Sports   Performing Arts

Outdoors   Exercise

Music   Mechanics

Art   Food

Gardening   Crafts

Collecting   Other

You will find more information about finding BALANCE in your life in Appendix A.

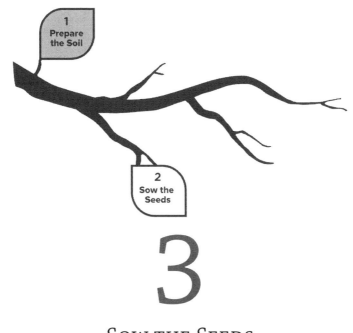

3

Sow the Seeds

O kay, you're doing it! You're still reading this book!
Now you've been introduced to the first two steps of successful and powerful personal development:

- Deciding to live intentionally
- Preparing the soil of your mind to receive new seeds of thinking that will produce new fruit in your life.

Now we are entering into more of the action steps of growth—the "how-tos." We've laid the groundwork, now it's time to start planting some new seeds. But you must remember: if you don't take the time to prepare the soil, even the best seeds won't be able to take root, let alone produce a harvest.

You may have heard that ancient story about a man who sowed good seeds in his field. But while everyone was sleeping, his enemy came and sowed weeds among the wheat, and went away. When the wheat sprouted and formed heads, then the weeds also appeared.

The owner's servants came to him and said, "Sir, didn't you sow good seed in your field? Where then did the weeds come from?"

"An enemy did this", he replied.

This is a great parable with some truly deep wisdom in it. I first read this story in the Bible (Matthew 13:24) in case you want to see how it ends.

The reason why I bring up this story is because of the way it confirms the fact that whatever you sow, that's what you're going to reap! Even if it's negative and even if you think "you didn't sow it". It's still going to grow up and reproduce itself.

I love the way the owner of the field is so quick to play the victim! Yes, it's unfortunate what has happened to him, but let me point out that HE PLAYED A ROLE IN HIS OWN TRAGEDY! Notice the story says, "while everyone was asleep"… This includes him!

This happens to all of us at some point - we don't pay close attention to the "seeds" that are being sown and while we're "asleep"… some junk gets tossed into our minds.

Just before our daughter, Clare, was born, Lisa and I decided to disconnect from the TV for a while. We turned off our cable and just used our TV as a monitor for our video recorder.

That lasted for 14 years!

Our family was hilarious when we'd stay in a hotel on vacation. We would be all glued to the TV like we had just been transported from the 1930's! Because we had such little connection with TV, we were able to see how technology and culture were racing forward. Everything was moving so fast on the screen.

Just this month, we finally caved in and got basic cable because we got tired of missing the Oklahoma Sooners football games!

Wow, the last shows I remember getting into were *Friends* and *Seinfeld*. Things have changed!

According to a Nielsen report that showed up in the New York Daily News (September 19, 2012) the average American over the age of 2 spends more than 34 hours a week watching live television! Wow! Americans over 65 average over 48 hours a week, or nearly seven hours a day!

The National Sleep Foundation reported (March 7, 2011) that 95% of Americans use some type of electronics like television, computer, video game or cell phone at least a few nights a week as they go to bed. Hmm? "While they were sleeping…"

Now, this book isn't meant to be an anti – TV book, but you may be interested in what comes up when you Google "most watched TV shows this year". I'm sure you'll see some "weeds" in the bunch. So, be aware of what you're planting in your brain! Pay attention!!

In this chapter, you'll learn how to choose seeds wisely and collect them for planting in your garden. We'll also cover how these seeds get planted, and then what to do once they are in the ground. Again, all of this is metaphor language for your successful personal growth. At this point, you have done a lot of work preparing the soil—it would be unfortunate, after all that preparation, to sow seeds that produce nothing, or that produce fruit you don't want in your life. Enough of the metaphor—let's get to the real stuff!

SELECT THE SEEDS WISELY

Seeds are the new ways of thinking—new ideas, new thoughts, and new perspectives. It's best to have an idea where you want go before you take off and start planting.

The Four Wheels Of Health we covered at the beginning of chapter two may have revealed some areas where you would like to begin planting new thinking into your life so you will have a chance to produce different results. You also may have decided on some specific areas to focus on as you identified some weeds and rocks in your garden.

What fruit do you want to grow? We can have a tendency to just start planting stuff. Information and education have become extremely important in our world. "Information Is power," as the saying goes, and it rings true in the culture I wake up in every day. It's no wonder when a person gets a notion to embrace personal growth, the first thought is, "*I need to learn more*"! Unfortunately, this can be a tragic first step in the wrong direction, sending us into a vast wasteland of artificial solutions.

Now, I'm *not* saying that we don't need to learn anything new. Obviously, that is not the case. But remember: we may need to stop to consider what we need to *unlearn* first! By the time we are young adults, there are so many inappropriate and even harmful conclusions in our paradigm—to just start learning more things without first rightly discerning what needs to be replaced, we can easily find ourselves on a path that *seems* to have all the makings of personal development only to discover we have simply been on a treadmill.

Some other reasons why people often start out randomly:

1) *It's a novelty*! It's cool and trendy, "I was talking with my life coach this morning and he said …"

2) *It's the something new to distract you from all the old*. "I just want things to change because I'm bored with a life that has become too predictable." This often involves an unreasonable shift that is difficult to sustain over any long period of time. When we aren't able to sustain the change, we accuse ourselves and find more reasons why we will always be stuck!

3) *You're in pain and you want it to stop, now!* If you're in the midst of a painful life circumstance, most often you just want to relieve the pain, so you start taking advice from anyone and everyone.

We listen to our pastor and our boss and our parents and our friends, the bartender and daytime talk shows and books and, and, and… we are so desperate, we'll take whatever we can get if it will stop the pain. The information may be good, but it's way too random to use in a positive way.

4) *You feel forced into the situation and just want to get it over with*! Something in life has happened, causing you to be very uncomfortable—you want to get it over with as quickly as possible so you concede to new ways of thinking just to get the pressure to go away.

Real personal growth is not something to just jump into without any forethought. Many life-coaching clients have come to me wanting to get rid of pressure in their lives. I talk to them about the results they're experiencing in life and how those are due to the way they think.

"Yeah, yeah," they say, "but I can't do this anymore. I need help right now!"

Most of these clients, after time, have wonderful discoveries of the inappropriate paradigms that are hindering their joy in life. But others just want the pain to go away and just stay with me as long as they are under pressure. I'm always amazed at how talented I am when a coaching client approaches me after just a month and says, "You have helped me so much. Thank you. I'll be in touch if I need you." *Wow, I'm awesome! I fixed 'em in just four weeks!* Unfortunately, that's very far from the truth—they were just focused on the pressure and neglected to go deeper to discover the cause.

So, it's important to take the time to discover which new thoughts need to be planted depending on the client's desired outcome and the particular season they're in. As I begin with a new coaching client, I always want to spend some time digging around to discover what healthy growth they already have in their life, what weeds, and how deep the roots are.

Once, a long time ago, I was in a particularly heated marriage counseling session with my first wife. We had been fighting for many weeks by this point. The counselor felt the important next step for us was to stand up and hug each other! That was *not* going to happen! This would be an example of the right seed (we probably *did* need to do a better job of loving each other) but in the wrong season!

PERSONAL STRESS QUESTIONNAIRE

On the next page is a short questionnaire I have used to help clients identify initial areas that may warrant some reflection and consideration for new ways of thinking. Completing this short survey may give you some direction on your first steps to take toward successful personal development.

PERSONAL STRESS QUESTIONNAIRE

Do You Currently Have Specific Career/Life Goals That You Want To Achieve?
Yes   No

Are You Satisfied With Your Movement Toward Fulfilling Those Goals?
Yes   No

What are your top three stressors (worries, concerns) over the past six months?
(Please Rank in Order 1-3)

___Work   ___Spiritual Development
___Marriage   ___Finding "Balance" In Life
___Kids   ___Health and Fitness
___Money   ___Feeling Out Of Control
___Not enough time!   ___Emotions
___Friends/Relationships   Other _____
___Personal Development ("I feel stuck!")

On A Scale of 1 to 10 (with 10 being the very best), how confident are you that your life is progressing according to your plan?

                    1   2   3   4   5   6   7   8   9   10   (Circle One)

On A Scale of 1 to 10 (with 10 being the best), how confident are you that you have the tools you need to help you achieve your goals?

                    1   2   3   4   5   6   7   8   9   10   (Circle One)

On A Scale of 1 to 10 (with 10 being the highest), how strong is the level of mentorship that you are receiving on a weekly basis?

                    1   2   3   4   5   6   7   8   9   10   (Circle One)

On A Scale of 1 to 10 (with 10 being the highest), how accountable are you being to completing the daily tasks needed to turn your dreams into reality?

                    1   2   3   4   5   6   7   8   9   10   (Circle One)

On A Scale of 1 to 10 (with 10 being the highest), what is your level of willingness to make changes in your circumstances?

                    1   2   3   4   5   6   7   8   9   10   (Circle One)

The "areas of pressure" are indicators where you may want to begin looking for new ways of thinking. The trap is to just think, *It has to be this way* or *It will eventually get better.* The truth is that your life will only change if you make the decision to change it. A car doesn't change directions on its own. Who's going to turn the wheel? And if you do turn the wheel, it only changes directions if you're in motion.

COLLECT THE SEEDS INTENTIONALLY

Once the type of seeds you desire to sow are identified, it is time to collect them. Where do you get these seeds? It's best to have a consistent source, especially at the beginning. Jumping from supplier to supplier can create havoc with your understanding and generate some very frustrating results.

Let me be sure this metaphor is clear:

- The seeds are the new ideas I need to adopt so I can navigate through my situation better.
- The source is wherever I'm going to get these new ideas
- My supplier is my mentor or the mentoring resource I'm choosing to tap to help me translate these new ideas into new actions.

In most cases, people never approach a mentor to receive new ideas. They simply try to plow through the problem with their limited mindset until the situation calms down, or until people finally begin doing what they want them to do. This is one way to do it, but it doesn't always lead to the best long-term results.

Do you have a counselor, a coach, or a book? What is the source of your new revelation going to be? There must be a reliable source and it cannot just be *you*! The source of new revelation must come from *outside* of you—this is part of the process of learning how to learn. If you could learn it all by yourself, you would never learn empathy and compassion for others. You would be self-sufficient and have no need for anyone else. This is the wrong path or, as Yoda might say, "the path to the dark side this is,"

Luke Skywalker had Yoda
Neo had Morpheus
Alejandro had Zorro
The Karate Kid had Mr. Miyagi
Even Kung Fu Panda had the little white fuzzy animal (I never was quite sure what that thing was!).

But the real question is, "Who do you have?" Who will be your Yoda? You won't get there on your own.

Would you believe me if I said that, without help, it's impossible to think anything other than what you already think?

I can't think outside of my box unless I have some help! That's the reason why I stare at my ceiling at night trying to figure things out and keep coming up with the same stuff! I keep circling around and around, without ever truly getting anywhere.

But I think that, if I just keep on thinking about it, I'll eventually figure it out.

Not so. Worry, stress, and confusion will continue if I just keep trying to figure it out on my own.

But it's the way we've all been programmed! We have been trained very well *not to ask questions*! You remember being in school? Who raised their hand after the teacher got through with the lecture and asked for questions? Even when the teacher had just gone over *genetic recombination*! We say, "I have no questions. It's all perfectly clear to me!" or we think to ourselves, *I'll just read and figure it out later*. Argh! We've been trained to just figure it out on our own. Well, how's that workin' for you?

You can't change yourself by yourself!

However, if we could be open to raising our hands and asking questions and bringing mentors, coaches, and counselors into our lives, questions can actually have answers! And then I could get some sleep and not have to stare at the ceiling so much!

Just like Luke Skywalker and Yoda, once you have chosen your guide, you must humble yourself and listen. I repeat: you can't do this on your own. You can only think what you think. It's going to take outside, objective thinking for you to navigate this growth and change. You are going to find, probably early on, that if you were to do it your way, you would do it differently. But you have to humble yourself and let someone else lead you in this. This journey was not meant to be traveled alone.

I totally understand that this mindset is very counterculture, especially here in the United States where our country was founded on a pioneer spirit. But, when it comes to business development, this type of thinking isn't foreign at all. Take a look at these stats on how mentoring has influenced leaders in the marketplace.

- 75 percent of executives point to mentoring as playing a key role in their careers. (Source: American Society for Training and Development [ASTD])
- CEOs state that one of the top three factors affecting career growth was mentoring. (Source: AccountTemps survey of Fortune 500 companies)
- 76 percent of Fortune 500 companies top 25 companies offer mentoring programs. (Source: Fortune)
- 96 percent of executives say mentoring is an important development tool. (Source: AccountTemps)
- Managerial productivity increased by 88 percent when mentoring was involved, versus only a 24 percent with only training. (Source: ASTD)
- 71 percent of Fortune 500 companies use mentoring to ensure learning occurs in their organization. (Source: ASTD)
- 95 percent of mentoring participants said the experience motivated them to do their very best. (Source: "The War for Talent" by Ed Michaels, Helen Handfield)

Mentoring and coaching is a no-brainer professionally, where we focus so much on what we do. But we somehow have a disconnect when it comes to using mentors personally, where the focus is on who we are.

INSPECT THE SEEDS CAREFULLY

There is an important step between collecting new wisdom and understanding and deciding to start putting into action what you've collected. You need to inspect all this new information to make sure it's worthy of adopting. You may *accept* it, but it is only after you have been willing to *adopt* it that you can have any hope to *apply* it with any regularity.

This step isn't difficult, but it's necessary. Simply inspect the new ideas. Make sure these new ideas are going to help you move forward along your journey. They may be good ideas, but are they helpful for you? Many people have been distracted from their life course by new ideas that were neat to think about but ineffective in moving them forward. Your mentor will need to help you maintain a proper perspective on these new thoughts.

It is very common for the life-coaching clients I work with to attempt to take on too much change all at one time, convinced this is the answer. However, for most, it's also the reason why they feel so overwhelmed! They say things like, "I can't do this anymore!" or "I'll never go back to that!" This obviously comes from a person who is tired of their current results and wants everything to change at once.

But drastic changes may cause more damage and pressure than necessary. Instead, having someone help you with perspective will be a tremendous benefit as you make decisions on next steps.

Remember, the journey is the thing! Today's destination simply becomes tomorrow's starting point! If you continue to think there is a place where you'll be able to say, "I've arrived," you're going to be consistently disappointed. At the very best, you'll arrive at a comfortable point, misinterpret it as the destination, and stay there, never pressing on to a greater measure of understanding and influence.

So it's important to pause for a moment after you ask questions in order to gain perspective on which new ideas to pursue immediately and which ones to hold for later. This is what allows you to live life in the midst of growing. The alternative is to feel like you have to stop your life and go off on some vision quest before growth can happen—and most people can't fit that in!

PLANT THE SEEDS DELIBERATELY

Now that we have learned some new thinking and determined a progressive path forward, it's finally time to plant the seeds! Let's start placing these seeds in the ground.

What does this look like?

All the material for mature fruit is found in the seed. You have to trust this natural law—if you doubt the seed has what it takes to make a mighty oak tree, you'll keep taking matters into your own hands and try to create it yourself. You'll try to act on a new idea before you really understand what it means. Yeah, good luck with that. You'll soon feel like you're trying to control something out of your control. This can make you feel like you're fighting with your life (or those in it) to try to get on top or get ahead… and you'll also feel like life is fighting back.

Practically, planting new ways of thinking can be done with your mentor, coach, or counselor either privately with just the two of you or publicly over coffee or lunch or anywhere that fits the situation. But a word of caution here: planting needs to be very intentional, deliberate, and consistent. Learning a new way of thinking and interpreting your life is a serious business. I have found that it *must* get on my calendar if it has any chance of actually happening. To just leave the next meeting hanging out there without a specific date and time most likely means it will seldom happen.

Here are five steps to follow:

Step one: Schedule several meetings at a time and get them on your calendar.

Step two: Meet for at least 60 minutes—it takes this much time to get to the heart of the matter. (I usually plan 90 minutes with each person I coach)

Step three: Stay focused on the new thinking you're trying to adopt and apply. It's easy to get distracted and talk about new problems, but I try to avoid these bunny trails unless the new problem is just another symptom of the old, inappropriate thinking.

Step four: Identify how the new way of thinking conflicts with your old reality. Admit that the new is different. Just don't make the mistake of thinking that different is bad!

Step five: Always include some action steps to take in regards to the new way of thinking. Start small at first and don't get discouraged if you're not able to be successful every time. Remember TFBAR—your thoughts will always lead to your actions. If you continue to struggle with specific action steps, it's simply because your new ways of thinking have not taken root yet. Be patient.

Along with meetings, I also recommend that you have specific supporting materials to help you walk through the process, like a reading list or journaling exercise or a prescribed set of CDs to listen to. These types of support materials help you stay with it. If you're not careful, you can fall into a trap of only working in your garden during your weekly meeting, but this just makes for slow growth along with a lot of confusing wild growth.

LEAVE THE SEEDS ALONE!

Now: *wait!* Don't try to act on things too quickly. If you do, you may get frustrated at your inability to follow through, which can lead to accusations coming from yourself and others about how nothing has really changed.

I used to do this all the time. I was always trying to help people (including myself) with the latest information I had heard. Some people would accept it at face value, but others would ask me questions about it. Unfortunately, because it had no depth in my thinking, I wouldn't know any answers. My defense would just be, "You should just believe it because I said it!" Yeah, that always went over real well!

It's in the waiting where you learn how to believe in the process. All that makes up the universe is not readily seen by the naked eye. At first, all growth is unseen and under the surface; let it happen undisturbed. Although you'll want to jump out quickly, be patient. This is where you will develop hope—a natural ingredient vital to all growth. A belief in the process allows us to hope; hope gives us depth and provides us with a foundation that allows us to weather storms. If we only put our hope in the final result, then our hope can be deferred for a long time, and that can "make the heart sick".

First put this new way of thinking in the ground and cover it up! Meditate on it and allow it to sink in. Ah! It's hidden! That's right. You can't see the very beginning, so don't get discouraged and think nothing is happening.

This is why you have to trust the process. If you have chosen a good master gardener (mentor, coach, counselor) then they will help you wait! Your tendency will be to act too soon, but this will only lead to pulling up new growth that hasn't matured yet. You'll want this new growth to fix your problem or you'll want to share the new growth with others (to fix their problem) but since it's not mature yet, it can easily fall apart in front of you.

Wait!

The old, protective seed coat has to soften and peel away. This coat is simply your resistance to adopting the new ideas and the conclusions of truth about how life is meant to work so you can experience joy, peace, and fulfillment. Don't focus on the growth—stay focused on the nurturing, which I'll cover in the next chapter!

Eventually a small shoot will appear! No, this is not the full plant. Although it's very exciting to see some early growth, don't confuse this with mature growth. Be patient! The pace will be crushing to your old junior-high mindset that wants immediate gratification.

Eventually a flower will appear! No, this is not the fruit you're looking for, but it's very encouraging! Don't force it! Be patient! Stay focused on the process and not the end product, even if the pain and loneliness are overwhelming.

Finally, out of the flower, the fruit will appear. Let it ripen on the vine. Don't pick it too soon.

Once it's ready to pick, *then* you can apply it to multiple situations in your life and begin to share it with others. Keep in mind, the fruit of a plant was never meant to be the source of life for that plant; it's intended to be a source for other living things. We'll talk about sharing your fruit later on in chapter six.

I call all of this the Wait Room Phase. And the purpose of the Wait Room Phase is to get stronger! Okay, that's actually the weight room, but now you understand the double meaning that I'm so cleverly introducing in this section.

Once the seed is in the ground, you have to wait.

It's gotta start out buried. You don't see the initial growth. But just because you don't see it, that doesn't mean it's not happening!

The waiting softens the outer seed coat that allows for the shoot to break out. The waiting will soften your rigid resolve to make this happen at some pace other than what's natural. The waiting will humble you, and that's why so few people actually make it past this point.

Really, most people don't feel like they have the time to wait for growth to happen. They didn't take the time, like I discussed in chapter one, to create space in their lives for change. They didn't get prepared. Waiting will prepare you for life!

Life is way too big for you and me to control, and the sooner we grab hold of that paradigm the better. Embrace the wait! Learn to find peace in the waiting… it's called patience, and without it, you will always get caught fighting against the pace of life. Life is much too big to be manipulated by my puny efforts to rush it so I can get to the next thing on my list.

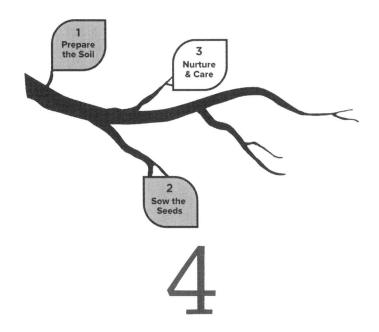

4

Nurture and Care for Your Growth

In the summer of 2002, Lisa and I moved our girls from Prairie Village, Kansas to Avant, Oklahoma to become the directors of Shepherd's Fold Ranch, a Christian Summer Camp and Retreat Center. We had been talking for months about the exciting times we were going to have training and developing college students while providing an incredible experience for hundreds of young campers each summer. When we arrived, I wasted no time in offering my expertise in leadership to over fifty young "twenty somethings". I called a meeting and began telling all of them how excited I was to bring "change" to their beloved (and sacred) campground. Yip, you guessed it. It didn't go over well! Within 30 minutes, I had turned all (yes – ALL) of them against me. My attempts to turn the ship too fast had split us right down the middle. I was sinking on one side and all of them were sinking on the other.

But I didn't give up! I continued to rally the troops! I had been on staff at this camp when I was in college and I knew how important it was to provide consistent encouragement and nurturing to the staff during those long, hot Oklahoma summers. So, I called another meeting

You know what?

NO ONE CAME! Not one person!

So I called another meeting and made it mandatory! Again, no one came!

Now, remember, I was the Executive Director of the company calling an "all staff" meeting and no one was coming. Hmm? I couldn't fire them all because we had already started the summer season and I had hundreds of campers on the way that would need these wonderful, older role models to emulate.

So I regrouped and told them that the meeting was going to be a discipleship training session, not a staff meeting (I was so clever!). I got ONE person to come! Her name was Lauren. It was her very first year to be on staff and she probably felt sorry for me. But she and I did the training together and we began to nurture those new seeds that were being planted in her heart and mind.

Wow, it was a very hard first few months on the job when the entire staff was vocally against me. I would have liked to have just "cleaned the table" and start over, but that wasn't an option at the time. I had to make it work with the team I had. It was very painful, but I didn't give up! I just kept nurturing the seeds (ideas) of a new way of thinking.

In the months to proceed, my time with Lauren turned into time with another and then another as the group grew. Within a few years, that time had become known as "Time With Clay" and to be invited to a seat around the table was a real honor. The "old guard" had moved on and I had brought in more and more employees that were compatible with the vision. "TWC", as we nicknamed it, grew and the discipleship training expanded to include leadership training and a ton of life coaching as we split the students into different groups according to their movement along the path we had designed for all of our employees. It was working!!

In the 2006 season, we had multiplied so much that we knew we had to make some changes. We had a waiting list of potential employees because we couldn't afford to pay them all. They were responding to the "nurturing"!

That's when I got a wonderful idea (*A wonderful, "awful" idea!"* from The Grinch).

What if we turned all this multi-level discipleship/leadership/personal training into a SCHOOL? And *charge* people to come rather than *pay* people to come!

We had spent four years sowing and nurturing into the lives of our employees with pigheaded determination and we had discovered that they had become extremely loyal to our company (and to us) because of the personal growth they were experiencing. I mentioned the idea to Lisa and she thought the idea might work. I mentioned it to a couple of business friends and they laughed and said no one would come and it would kill the business. But I didn't give up and neither did Lauren and the crew!

That following season we had a great team of about 35 veteran employees and I was very careful when hiring new people to make sure they had our cultural DNA -"*because I knew what I was going to be inviting them into at the end of the season*". With each training class I did for the next three months, I would always end with asking them, "So, do you think this training is valuable? Do you feel this time together is helping you grow as a person? How much do you feel like you're growing? Do you think you would have grown like this if you had chosen to work somewhere else? How much would this be worth to you if you were to put a dollar amount on it?" Their answers confirmed my suspicion – "They would pay for this!"

The seeds we had been planting and nurturing without giving up for four years began to produce a harvest! At the end of that season, we unveiled our plan to start a school called "The Furnace" and we would be charging rather than paying!

86% of the staff remained!!

And all but one of the others were heart broken because they wanted to stay but their life circumstances required them to move on.

As a business, we realized a 60% reduction in our staff expenses for the season. With this model we could accept and impact more people that aligned with our mission statement without creating a larger financial burden.

We had moved from no one showing up for a required meeting to over forty saying they were willing to pay for the meeting!

THIS IS THE VALUE OF APPLYING PIG HEADED DETERMINATION TO NURTURING SEEDS!

Each of those students were willing to REMAIN IN THE PROCESS and it culminated in the transformation of individual hearts and an entire company culture!

By the way, Lauren eventually became the Camp Director and an instructor in The Furnace! BOOM!

You see, all positive growth requires intentional and deliberate nurturing on a consistent basis. Healthy, productive growth rarely, if ever, happens on its own—you need "pigheaded determination" to see it through to the end. I'm talking about having the heart of a lion, but the mind of a pit-bull! My dad had a phrase that he used to say all the time when he would be teaching and training young "leaders-to-be". He'd say, "Never, never, never, never give up." I later learned that he was quoting the U.K. Prime Minister, Winston Churchill from a 1941 speech he gave to Harrow School. It was powerful.

The chapter you're about to read will actually equip you with very practical tools to help you maintain and nurture your personal growth. It's not rocket science! The steps you'll need to follow are exactly the same steps you would follow if you were nurturing growth in a garden. I'll provide you with the steps, but you'll have to provide the pig headed determination.

DO THE WORK!

You gotta stay with it! Remember this isn't just an *event*. You're learning a new lifestyle—a new way to live your life. This is bigger than just getting through some painful circumstances, and it's much bigger than just wanting to be a better person. This is about you becoming who you were created to be on this earth! This is big-picture stuff! Don't get trapped into reducing this process down to some kind of self-help program. This is much, much bigger than that! The work you'll do during this part of the journey will be so significant it will impact your grandchildren! I'm not joking! It could be significant enough to alter your family tree for generations, not to mention the impact you will have on countless other family trees because of your influence.

We've all seen the montage in a movie where someone reaches the point where they finally decide to do the work required for change. Suddenly, there are all these short clips, often set to a bouncy, Rocky-type pop song, of the person going through the process of change. Unfortunately, this part of the movie only lasts for about 45 seconds and then—*poof!*—the person is changed.

Even though the time frame is off, the idea remains true: it's always the big shift in the movie, where everything changes. You can feel the momentum shift and you have this sense that the person going through all this preparation is going to make it and reach their goal.

There comes a point in your life when you decide to do the work necessary to complete your goals of purpose and identity. That's what this part of the journey is all about. This is when you cross over and embrace the reality that your life is lived best when you submit to learning from it rather than just trying to control it.

When you hit this part of the journey you must lean on your resources for growth. Books, CDs, seminars, and conferences are all great, but nothing can beat the power and impact of another person—a mentor or coach—in your daily life to help you navigate the change you desire. Left on your own, this part of your journey will be extremely difficult.

Remember, you're not on this journey just to complete it—you're trying to learn how to *be* on the journey. You're learning how to learn. Your success on the path isn't just for you; it's vital to the success of all those who will be coming after you. You'll need to know how to mentor and coach *them*!

One of the key components to the success of the preparation is the willingness to listen to *and follow* the advice and leadership of your mentor or coach. I guarantee you'll come up with a thousand reasons why your mentor is wrong about what you should do next! They will tell you what to do and you'll just sit there and look at them and think, *This person is crazy. There's no way that's what is going on or that's what I'm supposed to do.* You may even go so far as to tell yourself that what they are telling you to do is not safe and that it would be foolish for you to follow their advice. You'll do everything you can to convince yourself that you know better.

Remember Luke Skywalker and The Karate Kid? They all had to get past a roadblock to their growth: the arrogance of self-reliance. Self-reliance is a trap when it comes to personal growth! Don't fall for it. You can go back to doing what you think is best, but remember, doing what *you* thought was best is what got you into this position in the first place! You can only think what you think!

To change, you must be willing to adopt new thinking and this new thinking, at the beginning, will be foreign and uncomfortable. It may even cause all kinds of inner alarms to go off, which is simply your old mindset trying to protect itself and maintain the status quo. You must trust your mentor! It's this willingness to release the reins and submit to someone else's leadership in your life that becomes the great lesson of this part of the journey. Those who refuse to do this will find themselves circling back into their own thinking and their own conclusions again and again. The change you desire will never seem to fully come and your frustration will continue to reside in your mind and in your heart.

For each of us to grow consistently, we must be able to recognize and receive food from each of the natural sources. In nature, healthy plants receive their life-giving resources from water, the sun, and the nutrients in the soil, all working together with the carbon dioxide that is in the air. From each of these sources, the plants are able to make food that allows them to survive.

Let's take a look at each of these sources as a metaphor for our daily lives.

WATER

This is new *information* we receive from books, workshops, articles, etc. as we daily pursue our personal growth. This isn't just information on how to do our job better and more efficiently (although it can include that), but its information on how to be a better you—how to become who you were designed to be. You will begin to build your library of resources that you can return to again and again—and that you'll be able to direct others toward in the future. Being "watered" like this will require creating space in your life that we discussed in chapter one.

A great time to "water" your garden can be while you commute to work each day—reading on the train or subway or listening to audio books or inspirational teachings in your car. Did you know that a study based on 24,861 people who participated in the American Time Use Survey found that more than one in ten people who had a full-time job spends two or more hours commuting to work!

That's twenty hours a week! That works out to close to 63 work days a year! That's like twelve workweeks of time spent each year in commute! Personally, my commute is almost an hour, and I make it three or four times a week. That gives me six hours a week (about 300 hours a year) to drink from the fountain of personal development! I think it's important to look at this on an annual basis. Looking ahead is a key component to personal growth. You have to get beyond just focusing on today and right now as you plan—that limited focus could easily keep you in survivor mode and keep you from creating the space you need.

If you're reading a book, I strongly suggest marking it up with your personal notes. I encourage you to underline and write in the margins and put big question marks by anything you don't understand. This creates great conversation fuel with your mentor as they help you make sense of the information your receiving.

Now, I know that some people hate to write in books, and that's okay. I'm a big "marker-upper" of the books I read, but if you don't like that, then simply replace it with some other form you enjoy (or that you can tolerate) that will help you *engage* in what you are learning. I simply mark the things that are speaking to me at that time. I may return to that book at another time and find something else standing out and then I'll mark it as well. The marking simply lets me know where I am on the path—like little GPS pins!

Some people have found enjoyment in taking advantage of all the digital technology that allows them to read, take notes, and even instantly share their thoughts with others. I love that! Again, the main thing is to have a way to *engage* with the new material.

Still others don't fancy themselves as readers and would rather *listen* to new information. This is wonderful, but it can be a little more difficult to identify key pieces of information speaking to you or challenging you unless you are taking notes while listening. I've had many occasions where I'll be listening to a CD in my car and will hear something I really like or that totally destroys one of my ways of thinking. How can I remember it without making a note? I have started doing one of two things: I'll use my smart phone to record a quick statement to myself about what I heard and what I think about it, and I often listen to the same CD over and over.

Another trap to avoid is always agreeing quickly with whatever you read or hear. If this is the case, you're either reading elementary books, or you're not processing while you're reading. Saying "yes" to everything will not help you grow in the midst of conflict. The information needs to be challenging and cause you to be stretched. Like lifting weights, if there isn't enough weight, your muscles will never grow no matter how much time you spend working at it.

I used to work as a trainer at an athletic club, and every day we had two women come in to work out for about three hours. They had all the gear and a seemingly good plan in place. They spotted for each other and encouraged one another at every station. Their form wasn't too bad and they seemed to have a good mix of free weights and machine weights. However, after working out this way for several months, there was never a change in either of their bodies! With all the time they were spending, nothing seemed to be changing.

I soon realized they were not adding enough weight. One day, I mentioned this to them and they replied, "No, this is the weight we want to stay at." I simply said, "Okay," and walked away. Their goal was to work out, not to change! (Read that line again. It's significant.)

Five quick questions may help you avoid this trap as you are processing. When reading or hearing new information, ask yourself:

1) Does this information challenge me? Why?
2) Where did I pick up the old thought that's being challenged?
3) Is that old way of thinking still valid for me today or does it hold me back?
4) Will adopting the new way of thinking help me move forward?
5) Are there other areas in my life that would be affected by this new thinking?

SUN

This is new understanding, not just more information. There is most definitely a difference between information and understanding.

I was a high school science teacher for 15 years; I *know* there's a big difference! In our global information infatuation, we still have tremendous difficulties and hurdles to overcome. Information, although very important, is not the complete answer to our woes. We must look *beyond* new information to begin to consider how we will interpret and then apply it. It's the very same in our personal lives. Information may be needed, but without understanding, the information can lead to confusion.

We've already talked in the previous chapter about where we go to get the right information and how to organize it, but information without proper interpretation is very dangerous. How many times have you been caught in a situation where you had some information that greatly effected your emotional life, only to find out that what you thought was true wasn't really what was going on. Or a time where you were personally accused of something because someone misinterpreted the facts. This is very common and very disturbing. Just watch any sitcom and you'll realize that miscommunication is the very basis of the plot... *and that's why we watch them*!

Because of this inherent dilemma with new information, it's imperative that we take the time to invest in the appropriate interpretation of any information we are taking in, to examine it and discover where and how it fits into our existing belief system. It may sound good, but if it doesn't ultimately agree with our foundational beliefs, then it will be only temporary.

I remember having a "light bulb" moment in regards to how I used to think about money. It hit me one day while I was driving. The understanding came like this...when I was seven years old, my mom and dad started a summer camp. We moved to the property in the country and they became the founders of the non-profit organization that would run the camp.

For the next 15 years, I was constantly surrounded by the non-profit world. As a result, I learned, from the models I had, how to *ask* for money. This was reinforced by the technique I acquired to raise my personal funds each week—ask Dad. I had learned, if you need more money, ASK FOR IT. (Note: This is a very noble and appropriate way for a non-profit organization to operate. However, it is a very poor model for your personal financial life.)

My next money indoctrination occurred in my early twenties when I worked an hourly job on the maintenance crew of a local country club. It was here where I learned how to *exchange hours* for money, doing that frustrating math to determine how many hours I would need to work if I wanted to make the money I needed.

Next came fifteen years as a salaried schoolteacher, where I learned how to *work hard* for money. The money was consistent, but it seemed the hours always got longer without an increase in pay. And, when I looked down at the bottom, right-hand corner of the pay scale, I noticed that even after 30 years of teaching, my salary would be way below what I wanted for my future.

These money mindsets were not going to get me where I wanted to go. Up to this point, all my decisions about where to live, where to vacation, what to buy, and what to give all had to fit within the limits of the money I had in hand (or would have in the next paycheck).

Side-note: My wife and I do a lot of Pre-Marital Counseling. One of the questions we ask when we arrive at the "Money Talk" is, "Let's say you need more money than you currently have in the bank for a certain new expense. How would you go about getting it?" Here are the top three answers we get:

1. Do without the new thing.
2. Ask someone (bank, friend, family member, credit card company) to loan it.
3. Work more hours or get a second job.

These three answers are most common. Keep in mind, most of the couples we counsel are in their twenties. These answers give us a very accurate idea of "how they think about money" and often lead to some very important discussion about their future. The point here is that their information is coming from a lack of understanding of how to support their desired lifestyle. They have information but need understanding.

As I began to contemplate becoming an entrepreneur and starting my own company, I knew these formative money mindsets would not fit. It took me over a year with my coach and many books and CDs (and out-loud, positive confessions each morning on the back porch), but I eventually learned how to think differently. I finally learned how to *make* money. "Light Bulb!" Now I get it! Making money is no longer this huge mystery and struggle. This *understanding* has allowed me now to *make* more in one hour than I had been making in one month! I now have a measure of understanding to go along with my information.

NUTRIENTS AND FERTILIZER (YES, I MEAN *POOP!*)

Embracing the daily poop and struggles that *will* come in life is a skill needed by all who are pursuing successful personal development. All the crap in your life is a wonderful source of learning and shaping for you—you just need to learn how to interpret it. Remember the equation A + B = C we talked about in chapter two? This is where interpretation is the key to positive actions and results.

My brother and I used to joke about a couple of proverbs out of the Bible: Proverbs 21:9, which says, "Better to live on a corner of the roof than share a house with a quarrelsome wife," and Proverbs 27:15, which reads, "A quarrelsome wife is like a constant dripping on a rainy day."

I don't mean to single out the wife here (I'm sure it goes just the same for the husband), but it sure sounds like Solomon had learned some lessons from some hard, practical experience. Did you know that Solomon had over 700 wives! I'm sure he had a *lot* of practical experience! Unfortunately, even though he was learning about what life was like with a quarrelsome wife, it doesn't sound like he was applying that knowledge to his life decisions! He just kept adding wives rather than realizing the problem was within *him*. Wow, can you imagine? 700 wives? Not to mention the 300 concubines! This is a wonderful example of learning a lesson, but not applying it to your life. Experiencing but never truly learning and applying will lead you to a pretty dark outlook on life. It did for Solomon—check out the book of Ecclesiastics.

It's only through the appropriate interpretation and application of these lessons that our lives are truly influenced and impacted (and changed). What have your life experiences taught you? Hopefully it's more than just, "I don't ever want to go through that again!" It's vital for you to investigate what role you may have played in the hurts and difficulties you've experienced.

(Note: I do not want to imply here that if you have suffered a hurt from abuse that it was in any way your fault at the time. However, if you have held on to that abuse and the vivid memories of it and it continually affects your ability to live your life today, I would contend that you may be experiencing that victimization over and over *now* because you haven't navigated through it and released it. You had no responsibility *then*, but *since then* you bear the responsibility of intentionally processing the event and moving on with your life, having embraced the lesson and released the wound.)

This topic of working through past hurts is a minefield because of all the different ways we have invented to conclude that difficulties and struggles in our lives were not our fault but the fault of some external force we were powerless to change. This is called victimization, and it is a subtle mole that burrows beneath the surface of our lives and eats away at any growing roots seeking for depth, nourishment, and stability. This way of interpreting the hurts in your life will continually leave you feeling out of control and fearful of any risks or leaps or anything other than the status quo.

These negative experiences and the hurts and pains that accompany them are very real and often very sensitive. The specific process of navigating through these experiences is much more involved than this book is designed for. However, you will find that if you apply the principles discussed in each of these chapters, it will put you on a path toward healing and freedom. I guarantee it! I've seen it happen far too many times to question this map! I know this map will get you there! Not everyone travels the same route, but everyone usually passes by similar landmarks.

I talked about poop in chapter three and I'll go into more detail of my personal journey later in Chapter 7. But in this section, I want to encourage you to consider how you have interpreted pain and difficulty in your life.

Some of my old hurts and interpretations were...

My Hurts	My Interpretations
Girlfriend breakup	Girls can't be trusted, so protect yourself from them
Getting fired	They don't like me and couldn't handle me
My divorce	I'm a failure (and I've screwed up my kid)
Family tension	They're all close-minded

This was how I had interpreted some of my hurts earlier in my life. Notice a lot of blaming my circumstances on other people. Yeah, that was pretty classic for me! How 'bout you? What are some of your life hurts? Did you ever take the time to process how you interpreted them? What did you learn? Did what you learned help you or hinder you? How did you grow as a result or did you shut down?

<u>**Your Hurts**</u>	<u>**Your Interpretations**</u>

I've learned to reinterpret those hurts! It took time and a lot of help from my mentors and coaches, but my new interpretations have set me free from being a victim all the time and feeling like I was always out of control and being tossed around and abused by this huge thing called life. I embraced new perspective on old hurts.

<u>**Old Hurts**</u>	<u>**New Interpretations**</u>
Girlfriend breakup	Humility—I was a selfish, controlling boyfriend
Getting fired	Humility—I was a bad influence on my students.
Divorce	Humility—I had an inflated sense of self
Family tension	Humility—I was a jerk and wouldn't listen

Wait a minute, there's a pattern here! Ha! I feel like I have become much more aware of my role in my circumstances and I hope to take more responsibility for that role.

To be a great leader, you must be willing to serve others and not just be served. I had to learn this lesson! It took a while because I didn't see or understand the process. Left to your own understanding, you're in danger of taking the long road to learn, but your mentor, coach, or counselor can help you stay on the path instead of getting distracted and heading down too many bunny trails.

Remember, you can only think what you think. And nothing dredges up impurities in our interpretations of life like pain and hurt, especially when another person brings it on. It took a lot of years and a lot of pain for me to become willing to embrace wisdom from someone else and admit I wasn't able to do it on my own. I had to make a pretty big mess of things first. Please don't make that same mistake.

CO_2

This is simply the atmosphere needed for healthy growth. *Your* atmosphere is made up of the people you surround yourself with, the attitudes you're exposed to, what you see every day, and the sounds you allow into your ears.

I've been in some pretty toxic atmospheres before, and I'm sure you have, too. The problem is that when I was in it, I didn't really recognize it. I thought it was normal. I had surrounded myself with people who were "like me" and so it all seemed so normal. Once again, this is where the objective thinking of a mentor, coach or counselor is vital for your healthy growth. Healthy seeds planted in good soil will never find their full potential unless they are in the right environment. The same is true for you! Take a moment to consider your "atmosphere." Is your environment encouraging you to grow, expand, and think differently, or is it filled with complaining, blaming, and name-calling?

The Greenhouse Effect

An imbalance in conditions involving water, humidity, heat, and air can place undue stress on plants and interfere with healthy growth. Even in the most favorable climate, soil quality, unusual weather conditions, bugs, and infestation can still pose a threat to well-tended plants. Creating a controlled environment where issues like water, heat, light, and air can be regulated allows for a stable, positive growing environment. The purpose of a greenhouse is to provide the *balance needed for optimal growth.*

It's fair to say that most people understand the basic idea behind a greenhouse and its value in growing plants. However, what is much less understood is the concept of using a greenhouse to grow *people*! Now it's not for lack of research or debate. Going all the way back to the 1300s—when the idea was first made public—to Francis Galton making it popular in the late 1800s, the Nature vs. Nurture debate still has no real conclusive findings. However, ask any parent and they'll tell you (and they probably did) to be careful who you hang around with.

"A man is known by the company he keeps." English Proverb

"If you hang out with chickens, you're going to cluck; and if you hang out with eagles, you're going to fly." Shirley Staires (my mom!)

To grow well, you must be very intentional about your environment, which is made up of the people you're with, the language you develop, the mindsets you form, and the ultimate scope of your influence on this earth. Your environment can either really help you or truly hinder you.

A greenhouse provides resources needed for healthy, balanced growth. Some of the elements of your environment may be out of your control—especially when you're young—which makes it all the more important for you to be diligent in maintaining a balance in your surroundings as you grow. It's hard to get a plant to grow if you never water it!

My earliest memories of childhood are in Tulsa, Oklahoma, when we lived in a great neighborhood with a ton of kids. This was *my* greenhouse. My best friend, Stevie lived next door. He was a year older and got me into so much trouble… anytime my parents grounded me, it was his fault! Stevie really influenced me and it seemed like any time I got around him, I didn't make good choices.

When I was seven, my family moved to Avant, Oklahoma, where I was introduced to an incredible greenhouse called Shepherd's Fold Ranch, the summer camp my parents started out on 90 acres in Osage County. Living at a summer camp offered me a wide exposure to people and experiences that helped me grow.

To this day, I'll never forget my primary role models were the counselors and staff at camp. They were all so cool and funny and exactly what I wanted to be when I grew up. And the chief among them all was my brother Mike. All these older kids gave me a future to look forward to. And what young boy wouldn't love to grow up on 90 acres with a barn full of horses? I'll never forget all the exploration and adventures I had with Shorty, my little Shetland pony—I even rode him to school and tied him up to the bike rack! It was this greenhouse that shaped my thinking and provided the balance I needed for optimal growth.

This culture stuck with me as I went on to high school and college. I didn't get caught up in all the junk that's so normal for kids. Things like drugs and alcohol just weren't an attraction for me—my idea of the party life was being with friends and laughing our heads off without the use of any controlled substances. By the time I went to college, my paradigms had been cemented that I was able to play college football and be in a fraternity without getting caught up in all the junk that becomes available to a young man in either of those groups.

The concepts in this book are like seeds that will take root and grow. However, it will take an intentional greenhouse for those seeds to produce an abundance of good, quality fruit in your life. It's going to take the help of others, and a strong determination from you to develop a healthy garden in your life where many others can be nourished. If you'll take the concepts discussed in this book and add them to a positive growth environment in your life both internally and externally, I can guarantee you a successful, abundant, and fulfilling life ahead. It won't be without difficulty and messes, but you'll even be able to embrace a little "poop" in your life!

What is the environment like in your home? At your school or office? In the break room or lunchroom? I remember some pretty toxic conversations in the teachers' lounge of a couple schools where I taught. In our own frustrations, we could get pretty nasty when talking about the students or the administration.

My daughter has recently launched out into the marketplace. The other day she made a comment to me about how mean the gossip and backstabbing was at her office. And she's only 21 and noticing this. This is the model of life in the workplace she's learning. She doesn't like it much! I don't blame her.

At this point, I'd like to take a moment to do a quick evaluation to make sure you're positioned to get the greatest benefit from this book. Answer the following questions on a scale from 1-10, with 1 meaning you disagree 100% and 10 being you agree100%. At the end, you can add up your score and get a decent idea of how prepared you are to grow.

How Healthy Is Your Greenhouse?

_____ I have the ability to choose and control my emotional responses to negative situations without engaging in self-destructive behaviors.

_____ I can read, write, and compute numbers.

_____ I have many role models I look to that have achieved what I want to achieve.

_____ I can fail without getting angry and blaming others or quitting.

_____ I have many friends I can talk to for encouragement to be successful.

_____ I know that I create my level of success; it's my responsibility.

_____ I have enough money to purchase the goods and services I need to grow in a healthy manner.

_____ I believe there is a divine purpose for my life and divine guidance to help me attain it.

_____ I have physical health and mobility.

_____ I know that I'm going to need help succeeding in life and that I can't do it on my own.

_____ I have friends and family and backup resources available to access in times of emergency.

_____ I have frequent access to adult(s) who are appropriate and nurturing and positive role models.

_____ I have knowledge of the unspoken cues and habits of successful people.

_____ **Total**

There's nothing magic about these scores. Scoring 130 points doesn't guarantee success, nor does a low score disqualify you from positive personal growth—this is simply an exercise to help you get an idea where your personal greenhouse may need some maintenance. I'm a teacher, so I instinctively go to a percentage on this and ask myself if I would be happy with that percentage on a test in school. In other words, any score below a seven should be addressed. The initial goal here isn't to get to a place where you have all tens; it is to become aware of where you are and then make intentional, wise decisions about how to proceed.

Remember, this book is a map! Have you ever tried to read a map without the initial information that reads: "You Are Here?" If you don't know where you are, it's very difficult to know how to get to where you want to go. It's this difficulty that causes many people to give up quickly after they begin.

I remember trying to give directions to my 16-year-old daughter soon after she got her license. She would call and say, "Dad, I'm lost," and proceed to ask me how to get someplace.

I would simply reply, "Honey, where are you now?" (notice the fatherly tone.)

"I don't know."

You can see the dilemma!

The natural greenhouse, where we grow plants, is so valuable because of its ability to stabilize the external and internal conditions of the soil and plant life—the same is true of our personal development greenhouse. There needs to be a proper balance of internal conditions (thoughts) and external conditions (relationships and life circumstances) to ensure healthy growth.

I think we would all agree with this but when it comes to personal development, so many people overlook this one key element: like attracts like. As a high school teacher for fifteen years, I always cracked up laughing on the first day when the entire class would segregate itself into small groups of "like me". Whether it was by race, gender or interests, it would always happen without fail. Then I'd bring out the seating chart and everyone would groan because of the forceful change they knew was coming. Fear would grip the kids as they thought about the dreadful possibilities that lay just ahead of them. Of course, they didn't see it as fear. They just got mad, complained, rolled their eyes, and made empty threats to other classmates as well as to me, their teacher. Eventually everyone would settle down and we would move forward with a new norm that some would accept and others would not.

This book may be the equivalent of a new seating chart for you. You may groan and complain, but you may find a freedom you never knew before. You'll discover the answer to questions that have plagued you for years. Whichever response you have initially, I strongly urge you to stop and take a moment to commit to getting to the end of this map! To stop prematurely is to stop short of the true destination and miss the whole point of personal development. The true destination of this map is to learn how to live in the process, because the process is what we call "life!"

Remember, everyone wants the rewards of growth, but not all are willing to embrace the responsibility required to attain them. Will you become that person? You *can* do this! You're still reading! Maybe you're even underlining things and keeping notes in the margins. *Don't stop!* Keep moving forward! Keep Growing!

PESTICIDE

If you apply each of these nutrients to your life, you will find they produce a natural pesticide for you. This chapter has covered four primary ingredients you'll need to produce a natural pesticide that will protect you from all the negative thinking and attempts to get you to settle for the status quo:

1) Embracing continued education and becoming a lifelong learner.
2) Interpreting and applying new information with the right understanding.
3) Learning how to correctly process the difficulties and struggles in life.
4) Surrounding yourself with a positive environment.

These four principles, intentionally applied with pigheaded determination, will provide a protective barrier for you against all the negative junk that so easily entangles you and makes life seem so hard. These four principles will also protect you against the inner voices as well as any of the voices you hear from friends or family members that attempt to discourage you from growing and moving forward. This natural pesticide can help create a protective barrier from the old junk coming back! Without all these in place, it's just too easy to slip back into the old ruts of our old mindsets. Your mentor/coach will help you avoid this classic trap.

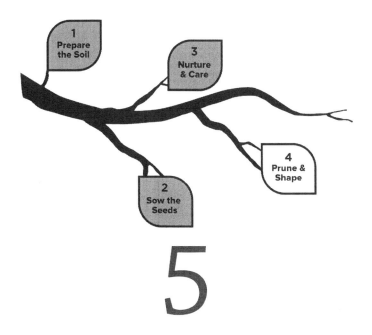

5

Prune and Shape

You're doing it! You're growing and it feels freeing! New thinking is producing new results in your life! But you know there could still be more—how do you get there? (I'm talking about the path here, not just the time it's taken you to get this far in the book.) Even though you may be experiencing some "light bulb" moments and hopefully are beginning to believe that successful personal growth is not the mystery you once thought it was, you're on the path and the path is ongoing.

This chapter is about the most difficult part of your journey, where your relationship with your mentor is going to be truly tested. Will you trust them? Chances are very good that eventually you're going to need to eliminate from your life specific things you have become quite attached to and that you have come to believe are "good things". This can even be some of the new thinking you learned along the way. It fit for the time, but now it's time to trim it back and refine it.

This pruning process is not to be confused with the initial clearing you did at the very beginning of this journey. Eliminating the substances from an abuser isn't pruning—it's a clear cut! At the beginning, we had to clear out space and eliminate obvious barriers so we could have some hope of success in growth.

After that initial clearing has taken place, we move on to preparing the soil and planting the seeds. Before long you will start to experience new growth: your responses to life are different; you have more patience with life because you've learned how to wait; your relationships with others improve because you have new skills in interpreting your circumstances. Peace, joy, and fulfillment will begin to grow in your life and you'll begin to enjoy and appreciate the new growth.

However, at some point along the way, you'll notice that some of your new growth is being influenced by some of the old patterns of thinking. You will most likely even discover some of the old thinking patterns attempting to weasel their way back into your life. So what's the answer? What's going on?

Pruning.

When I talk about pruning, I mean trimming and shaping the new growth. But, as we discussed earlier: left to ourselves, we just don't have the capacity to discern between healthy growth and wild growth. We're just too close to it, especially at this level of growth, where what is mostly needed is pruning and shaping rather than just some basic weeding and removing of stones.

First of all, let's take a look at our metaphor for a moment:

Pruning is perhaps the least understood and most abused of all gardening chores. Many people prune their plants for the same reason some men climb mountains… because they're there. They stand in the doorway of their garden shed with loppers and a saw in hand like some

Texas Chainsaw Massacre movie, with little knowledge of the plant's ideal form, the best time to prune, the proper way to make a pruning cut, or when to stop. Incorrect pruning results in poor growth, unnatural plant forms, and poor flower and fruit production. (Wow, that's a great metaphor!)

This is a very difficult phase of personal growth because of the level of trust required between you and your mentor, coach, or counselor. I would suggest that the best time for pruning in personal development is *not* when you're experiencing some major pressure and stress in your life. At that point, many times you're just dealing with the (negative) fruit that's right in front of you. Pruning is best done during times of rest with a view toward future fruit. That's why it's tough… and why so few people ever make it successfully through this part of their development and, as a result, remain limited in their ability to process new levels of expansion in their life.

Pruning will introduce you to language like: dysfunctional, inappropriate, harmful, diseased, wild, abusive, eliminate, submit, obey, no, now, counseling… all the words we don't really like to associate with our daily lives. In fact, many people would contest that these words even coincide with the concept of growth; they sound more limiting than freeing.

Why Prune?

When we prune a plant, we should have a specific purpose in mind. Pruning just because it is pruning season is not a good reason for pruning. What *is* a good reason? Some include shaping plants, removing dead and damaged branches, and containing plants that are outgrowing their area. Shade trees are sometimes pruned to raise the lower canopy or to correct a poor structure. Are you following the metaphor here?

Plants may be pruned to improve flower production. Fruit trees are pruned to increase new growth and fruit formation. Pruning an old plant can help rejuvenate it and encourage new growth. Are you tracking with this?

Pruning finds its primary purpose in *training* a new tree, shrub, or vine. When this is done properly, it eliminates virtually all pruning later in the life of most trees. In fact, in most cases if you are using a saw (rather than loppers) on a landscape plant, it is usually an indication that a poor job of training was done early in the life of the plant. Wow, that is such a rich metaphor!

By cutting back a little, you increase the chance for healthier, stronger parts to grow.

When a tree is pruned, only particular portions are removed. These portions may be removed because they are dead and there is a risk they might fall and injure someone. They might be removed because they are damaged or diseased and are affecting the overall health of the tree. Additionally, a healthy tree might be pruned so that a portion of it can be transplanted to another area. Whatever the reason, pruning a tree should improve the health and condition of the plant, and should be undertaken with care and planning.

So, how does the pruning process work? Let's take a closer look

IDENTIFY INHIBITING AND INEFFICIENT GROWTH

It can be very difficult, if not impossible, to see where you need to prune or weed *yourself*. Remember, we're not talking about the initial stages of growth when you needed to clear out obvious and specific inhibiting factors in your life. An alcoholic needs to stop drinking; the substance abuser needs to cut out the substances.

But later on in the process, when you start seeing new growth that is inefficient or even harmful, you have to be able to expose the *reasons* for it and begin eliminating it from your life. It's not just *what* you think, but it's *why you think it*! Some of these mindsets may be very dear to you, but you'll have to lay them down so new thinking can find a sticking point and you can move forward in completing your design and purpose on this earth.

During this part of the growth process, you'll need a trusted and knowledgeable person to help you identify and eliminate this inappropriate growth. Most often, the ways of relating to life and to others are so subtle we don't even recognize when something is dysfunctional or inappropriate.

You will learn how to find a mentor later in this chapter.

SHAPING: SUBMISSION TO AUTHORITY

The language and process of pruning and shaping can be offensive if we're not yet ready to let go of some of our dysfunctional thinking. In fact, there *will be* situations where some thought is brought up for pruning and you will look at it and say, "Not that one! I've always thought that way! I don't think it's dysfunctional! I don't think you truly know what you're doing. I think I know better!"

Boom! There it is. *I know better.*

That single phrase will inhibit your growth more than anything else. Trust me, I've been there. It was through the pruning process that I discovered the value of submission to authority in my life. Up until my early thirties, I was pretty much the one in control of my life. Even as a young kid and teenager, I resisted anyone telling me what to do. I was a horrible student in the classroom if a teacher attempted to shape me—I once got three licks from Mr. Needham in seventh grade because I wouldn't say, "I'm sorry" to a classmate. Then I got three more because I walked off with a smirk on my face! No one was going to tell me what to do! I would shape myself! (By the way, "licks" were spankings in the office with a paddle! It was swift justice that only caused pain and discomfort to the one who had done the crime. I was a frequent customer both at school and at home.)

In high school, I made a teacher cry when she tried to control me and I refused to submit to her. She was new and didn't yet know a lot about classroom management. One day, I had become so frustrating to her that she started crying and had to leave the classroom. You may be saying, "Clay, you were a punk!" And I would totally agree with you, now. But back then, *I was justified* because I *knew better* than anyone else!

In college I actually told a professor, *the Dean of the school*, to just let me know when the tests were, that I would come for those because I knew I could teach myself better than he could! Yes, I said that! Of course, you can see the train wreck that was headed my way, but I didn't. I was blind to my own "punkness!"

I got fired from a job, but that was just because my *dad* didn't understand what a genius I was! I was just trying to help him grow the family business by offering my advice as to why he needed to do things my way and not the other way around. Ah! Even now, I can't believe that I didn't see all this in my attitude. I was so blind.

This issue of submission to an authority in your life must be settled if you want to survive the journey of developing into your full capacity and achieving the ultimate impact of your design on this earth. I'm not talking about just obeying your boss and making sure you get to work on time—I'm talking about submitting to someone in your life who is telling you how you should live, even when it goes against what you have always thought. Now this is where many people will stop reading the book! *What if they tell me to go jump off a cliff?* Well, if you have chosen a wise mentor, even though "you feel like" they're asking to you jump off a cliff, you better get to jumpin' because there's probably a good purpose behind it!

The point is that most people, including me, want to be in control. We don't want to subject ourselves to someone else because we don't want to lose that control, so we use extremes like, "What if they tell me to go rob a bank" as intellectual reasoning to justify our prudent thinking! Really?

This is what I did, and it's what I encounter quite often as a Life Coach. At some point, most people, after getting through some of the initial pain and confusion of growth, begin to say, "I think I can take it from here." They see new shoots of understanding emerging from the ground and mistake them for mature growth.

This pruning piece of the process is hard, and most people don't make it through. They suddenly discover a newfound mentor, or have a revelation they have completed the process, or something distracts them and becomes more of a priority. Don't let this happen to you. Stay focused! Don't lose sight of the goal of fulfilling your complete design! Remember: this isn't just an event in your life; it's learning a new lifestyle—a way of interpreting your life and your daily circumstances.

You can't do it alone.

Before my first marriage, I had many of my friends and family members questioning me about the wisdom of my choice for a bride. She was a darling gal, but just had a lot of, well, "struggles". Other people saw these struggles and attempted to warn me. But I didn't see them as struggles! I saw them as opportunities to prove to the world my AWESOMENESS! I was going to *fix* her. The more "struggles" she had the better I was going to look when I rescued her. Wow, when I finally had my eyes opened to my lack of submission to authority in my life, it's hard to believe she stayed with me as long as she did. The whole relationship was designed to meet my needs!

I'm sure you know just what I'm talking about here! If you haven't been in this type of relationship, you know of someone who has. Get them a copy of this book and tell them it will save their marriage!

BREAK OUT THE CLIPPERS: RESPONDING TO CORRECTION

Continuing with my own life experiences… because I resisted submitting to any authority in my life, anytime someone would correct me, I would lock up and shut down. If they continued to press the issue, I would get sarcastic and mean, doing whatever I felt I needed to get them to back off. I had such a strong need to be right that the mere consideration I could be wrong would send me into a rage. "How dare you challenge me"! Looking back now, it was ridiculous. But back then I didn't see it.

You see, if you're unwilling to submit to any voice other than your own, you will never respond well to correction unless it comes from yourself and, like we've already discovered, we don't always see our own flaws very well. This concept of submitting to authority and responding to correction is much bigger than the scope intended in this book, but I definitely want to touch on it because it's such a vital component of personal development.

I always used to interpret correction as people telling me I was stupid and not a good leader. A short comment of correction would put me in full-on defensive mode, lobbing insult grenades from behind my emotional barricade. Their intent wasn't to attack me but, because of how I interpreted the comment, that is how I would respond.

A + B = C!

How do you learn to respond well to correction? Submit and humble yourself.

Once you have all the pruned clippings lying on the ground, don't try to grab one and graft it back in to the tree! Commit to not going back to your old thinking and put the protective barriers in place I talked about in the last chapter. This word, "commitment" is another word that seems to be fading in value in our culture. However, without commitment, there can be no fulfillment!

SUPPORT THE VINE: HOW TO CHOOSE A MENTOR

Finding an actual person to help you *navigate* through the challenges life throws at you can be a very difficult task. Many people would love to have a Yoda in their life, but don't know where or how to find them.

The best way to summarize what to look for when searching for a Mentor is the acronym **FRUIT**

Do they have…

1) Fruit that I want to have in my life
2) Respect in the community
3) Understanding of the process of personal growth
4) Intentionality in relationships with people
5) Time to give

These qualities don't guarantee anything—they just let you know you're on the right path. On a scale from 1-10, you'll want your mentor to be able to score at least a 7 or better on each of these areas.

The *Fruit* lets you know what will be reproduced in you.

The *Respect* lets you know they are sharing their fruit with others.

The *Understanding* lets you know they will know how to respond to you when you fail.

The *Intentionality* lets you know they are serious.

The *Time* lets you know they are committed. If it's not on the schedule in today's crazy world, it's probably *not* going to happen.

Once you have found someone you would like to talk with, ask him or her out for coffee. (Note: there is a lot of wisdom in a female having a female mentor and a male a male mentor. It avoids a lot of confusion.) Do a short interview with them. Tell them you have notice the fruit in their life and would like to know them better. Ask several questions about their life. *Be sure to ask!*

- How did they learn to make choices?
- What has been their hardest season?
- Have they ever mentored someone or helped someone through a hard time in his or her life?

If they say no to this last question, they may not be the best choice and you can simply continue talking without ever asking them to mentor you. This will avoid any awkwardness if the person isn't able to be your mentor. By doing this, you are preparing them for the invitation. This is a smart thing to do.

If they have mentored someone before, you can ask follow-up questions about what that was like:

- Did you like it?
- What did you do?
- How did the "mentee" respond?

This way you can get an idea of what it may look like for you, and then you can decide if you want to ask them. If it all looks good, tell them about where you are in your life and that you need some help navigating, then ask them if they would be willing to be your mentor.

Don't expect to fully trust them right away, that will come as you develop the relationship. However, a tree is known by it's FRUIT. If they have the FRUIT you can relax and allow yourself to trust them.

Final word of advice, if there is *no one* in your life who has this FRUIT … you may want to consider expanding your relationships so there are several people to choose from.

Remember… no one is perfect so don't wait too long.

Okay, one more final word of advice…

Mentoring is what I do for a living and with every person I mentor, I immediately ask them what they are doing to help someone else? If they aren't doing anything to serve others then I usually ask them to go do something and then come back when they have questions. People are changed in the forge of responsibility! If the person isn't doing anything, I have found it just doesn't work out well. I guess this also follows the ancient principle of sowing and reaping—if you want to reap a mentor, you should probably start sowing as a mentor.

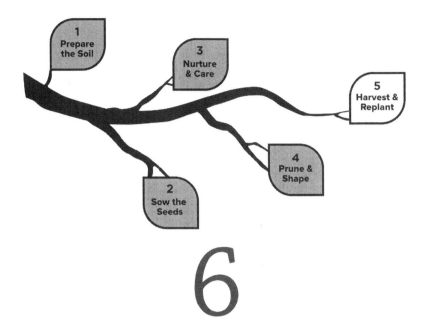

6

HARVEST AND REPLANT

We've finally gotten to the place where the fruit of all our labor in personal development begins to mature! This simply means that it begins to grow naturally without so much effort and energy. Like riding a bike without having to focus so much on maintaining your balance, this is a time of living with an increased capacity to understand ourselves, and the events that go on around us. So few people ever make it to this point in their personal development.

However, just getting to this point has never been the ultimate goal. Remember, we are striving to achieve the ultimate purpose on this earth that we were designed to have, and that ultimate impact will never be fully realized without using what you have learned to help others achieve their ultimate impact! John Maxwell says, "There is no success without a successor." Jesus Christ said, "If you want to be great, learn to be a servant."

The purpose for the new fruit in your life will always be to share it with others and not just use it all for yourself. People will notice how you engage and respond to life with peace, joy, and fulfillment and it will attract them to you. This is your fruit—and so many people out there are very hungry!

What will you feed them?

You'll feed them yourself – the encouragement you've discovered in your story!

I have been so blessed to be able to offer my story of encouragement to others in the midst of their difficulty. I have been fortunate to be able to communicate this encouragement and coaching through a variety of resources like books, cd's, life coaching, online video coaching, business consulting, and a host of programs designed to equip people with the tools necessary to grow personally, professionally and spiritually. Each of these resources is a "fruit" of labor I have spent the last 20 years embracing and nurturing. This fruit continues to provide "food" for thousands of people every day as well as an "income" for my family. The point here: "YOUR STORY HAS VALUE".

This chapter is written to help you discover that value.

INSPECTION

How do you know what "seeds" have been developed in your life? How do you discover what you have to offer?

Well, let's begin with taking a look at the things you have learned through your life experiences that will be helpful to others. How did you learn it? What were your struggles? What common pains and hurts occurred in your life that others will relate to? How did you process those pains and hurts?

All these questions will help you dig through your story to discover who you are and how you got that way, which is imperative to your personal development. But it's also vital to discovering how your story can be used to help others. Most people walk around everyday with a very shallow understanding of their identity and even more of a misunderstanding of how they got that way. This lack of understanding leads to a shallow foundation that constantly feels the pressure of all the outside forces that stress us out each day.

Just like you may thump a melon in the fruit aisle at the grocery store, it's important for you to inspect the "fruit" coming out of your life. Other questions would include: how do you tend to influence people each day? What kind of words do you choose when speaking to others? How do people feel when they're around you? How peaceful is your mind as you lay down at night? If someone were to "become like you," would that be a good thing for a lot of people? Would you be proud of that person?

Inspection may take some time to learn. Don't just assume you will know how to do it because you're an adult. Let your mentor help you with an objective perspective that encourages growth. For example: one day at the grocery store my mom asked me why I chose a specific tomato. Up to this point, I thought that the best tomatoes in the bin were the hard ones—she told me that was true with apples, but not with tomatoes. The best taste comes from the tomatoes that have just a bit of tenderness to them as you squeeze them. Boom! I was learning how to inspect the fruit from an avid pro and not just leaning on my own youthful understanding!

COLLECTION

What did your path look like? Can you organize your story into a road map for yourself? It may not be how everyone else will do it, but it's how you did it. What are the overarching themes of your life and journey? Were there patterns in your story? Are there lessons for others to learn from your story?

One tool I use and have shared with many of my clients to help them begin to "map" their story is an exercise called The Sticky Note Timeline. You will see the result of this exercise in Appendix C about Writing Your Story, but let me quickly explain how this exercise works.

Sticky Note Timeline Exercise
(Developed by Terry Walling. Used with Permission)

Most people feel their lives are commonplace. It is not until we take an in-depth look at our lives that they begin to recognize how we have been formed and shaped. This exercise will help you see the "process" that has made you who you are today.

You can use a poster board 14 inches x 22 inches and small 2" x 2" sticky notes of different colors to design a timeline of significant events in your life.

Many people, events, and circumstances have been used to shape your life. Take some time to reflect back from through your life and recall significant shaping experiences.

As you reflect, think of:

- The **events** in your life that influenced who you are today.
- The **people** who influenced and shaped your life.
- The **significant circumstances** that affected your life direction.

Shaping experiences can be *positive* as well as *painful*. Both types need to be seen and considered.

Step 1 – Capturing Your Life Experiences

Take the yellow pad of sticky notes and capture one event, person, circumstance etc. per sticky note. Write a few words about each event or person that will sufficiently describe the impact of this experience. A goal would be to try and create as many as 30- 50 sticky notes. Sometimes the most seemingly insignificant memories come to mind, go ahead and write these down. If they prove to be insignificant you can discard them later. Stack the sticky notes in front of you on a table, or on a piece of paper without concern for order at this time. Use only the yellow sticky notes as you capture these experiences.

Step 2 – Separating Your Life Experiences

Not everything in life is positive, painful events are part of every person's journey. The next step is to transfer every event, person or circumstance on the yellow sticky notes that were painful or negative, to a pink sticky note. The test for whether it goes on a pink sticky note is if *at the time you experienced it*, it was painful or negative. When you have transferred a negative experience to a pink sticky note, discard that yellow sticky note.

Step 3 – Organizing Your Life Experiences

In the next step, transfer your sticky notes from the tabletop to the poster board (or an open file folder) while putting them in chronological order. When doing this, leave a 1"-2" margin at the top and a 2" margin at the bottom.

- Use the whole poster board. You don't have to jam everything to one side.
- Earliest note top left
- Integrate pink and yellow as you go

- When you arrive at the margin on the bottom or you find the next sticky note represents a whole new chapter of your life, start a new column.
- You may still remember missing events - add those notes as you go - yellow or
- pink.

Step 4 – Identifying Chapters in your Timeline

In each person's story there are chapters, distinct endings and beginnings. Chapter titles can be as creative as you want. Some people have used TV shows, sports themes, and other metaphors. In this next step look and try to find five to seven chapters in your timeline, you may have to rearrange some of the sticky notes and that's fine. Identify the chapters in your life with blue sticky notes. Place the blue sticky note at the top of your poster board identifying each chapter.

Step 5 – Life Lessons

We have often heard it said "experience is the best teacher." I submit to you that "evaluated experiences are in fact the best teacher." Many people feel they have nothing to offer as they have had many experiences, but have not reflected to learn what lesson they were to have learned from that experience.

Look at each of your chapters and try to identify one or two lessons you learned or conclusions you adopted. Place these on green sticky notes and place these chapter life lessons at the bottom of the poster board under the chapter where you learned them or where they originated.

Step 6 - Summarizing your Life Lessons

I'm sure you have learned some powerful lessons and forged some important values through your life experiences. This final step is about crafting your life lessons into an orderly pattern that allows you to learn from them and communicate them better to others. Here are some examples from my life -

Life Lesson Examples: from my story…

Family – If I gain the world but lose my family, I am nothing.

My uniqueness – I am designed to help people navigate the thoughts and emotions that accompany change as they ascend to greater measures of influence in their lives.

Team – We enter into more when we enter in together.

Pain – I learn the best and the most through struggles and difficulties.

God - God is good and doesn't leave and he desires to have a personal relationship.

Leadership – To lead is to serve.

Life lessons are things you've paid a price to learn. Is it possible for you to be a better steward those lessons by intentionally, boldly and appropriately sharing them along the way, more and more often?

So, how 'bout it? What are you're life lessons? I've provided a few "sample topics" to start with, but you should add to it. What conclusions have you drawn about each of these categories based on the interpretation of your life story?

This is one way you can collect the "seeds" to begin sowing into the lives of other people.

Family –
My Destiny/Purpose –
Pain –
Life –
Love –
God –

Storage Of Your Fruit And Seeds

Journaling. Write it down. You don't necessarily have to focus on the past. Just start today and write from this point forward. You can fill in gaps later. How to journal? What keeps us from journaling? What are the consequences of not keeping track of the path? What is the legacy of your story? When you write it, you own it. I talk more about journaling in Appendix B.

Sharing

It's not all for you! You have to spread it around! What you cast out will return to you. Pay it forward. The great cycle of life. It's better to give than to receive. Teaching it will ground it in you. All of these are wonderful clichés that emphasize the importance of sharing our lives with others. Now you have a message to share with the world. I guarantee there are thousands of people who would benefit from hearing the wisdom you've gleaned from your inspection of your life. There is a book inside of you that only you can write! Today, there are so many people looking for answers to questions that overwhelm them. You can be a part of the solution by sharing your education, experience and evaluation with others in your sphere. If you don't share your story, there will be people out there that will have to learn it the hard way and it could take them a long time. YOU CAN HELP! Your story is meant to be shared!

Saving for Replanting

You'll eventually find a balance between what you have learned and what you can share. You can't lead where you won't go, and you can't teach what you don't know. Your language will change. You will be very deliberate and economical with your advice. You may know but that doesn't mean you will automatically tell. There will be some lessons you are still working through personally. There will be some lessons you will continue to struggle with, even though other areas of your life are growing so well. Your life will become concentric circles rather than a linear path, expanding evermore into the full capacity of your ultimate design.

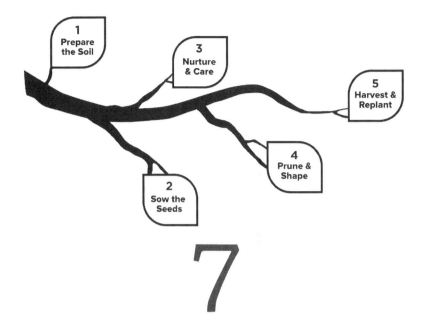

7

A CALL TO THE FIELD

IT's TIME TO REPLANT

Once you create your map, you'll find yourself adding to it often. Memories will surface, understanding will come, and necessary pruning will become a mainstay in your life. You will experience massive and speedy growth as you gradually come to understand the *bigger story* of which you're a part! I assure you that, at some point during this stage, someone will come up to you with a question about his or her path. They will explain a situation with which you will be very familiar and they will ask you for advice, counsel, wisdom or answers. *And you'll realize you've been there and know the way through!*

You'll know, at that moment, that your life has purpose and it's not just about you reaching your own goals. You will discover that the greatest joy in life is helping other people reach their goals! You will simply tell them your story and ask them if anything fits or makes sense. I guarantee you that people will be waiting in line to spend time with you! *Tell your story*!

The great thing in all of this is that you can be growing strong in one area in your life and still be just a seed waiting to be planted in another area of your life. I say that to encourage you that you're not just one big ball! You have many different aspects of you all growing at the same time and at different rates. And, yes, there are probably seeds in your life that are still to be sown. Just because you're 76 years old, doesn't mean you're done! As I write this, my mom, Dr. Shirley Staires, is 77 years old and is *still* looking for the next thing she can do to impact her life and the lives of as many others as possible. I love that role model! And I love my mom!

You may have a long way to go in some areas of your life, but I'm sure there are other areas where you have been able to conquer. Can you identify those areas? How did you learn to conquer that area? Is it possible, over the next couple of months, for you to meditate on the process that brought victory to that area, to the point where you could draw your map? I encourage you to work on this. Start drawing your map! Just like any map, there are many starting points and many destinations—I challenge you to begin to discover what those are. I challenge you to act on what you've read in this book. I know that if you do, then your life—and the lives of many people around you—will be dramatically changed for the better!

SO THEN, HOW SHOULD I LIVE *TODAY*?

Too often, as a result of our culture, we strive for "fruit" before we have done the preparation. It's the classic "fast food culture" you have heard about that has trained us to think, "I shouldn't have to wait". But successful personal growth takes time even when you're doing everything right!

You have to imagine yourself as a successful farmer. Take a look at each of the steps that we've covered in this book using the metaphor of planting a garden.

1. Clear and Protect the Area
2. Prepare the Soil
3. Sow the Seeds
4. Nurture and Care for the Growth
5. Prune and Shape the Growth
6. Harvest the Fruit and Replant

How do these metaphors apply to our lives on a daily basis? As you navigate the metaphor, you will get a very clear picture of how we are to live out your daily lives today. It will simply depend upon which "step" you're in. Unfortunately, most people try to live every day in the step of Harvesting Fruit. You can easily jump to the conclusions that you have to produce good fruit immediately. But what if you're at the very fist step? Are you still required to produce the good fruit that's expected at step 6? If not, then how should you then be living? Way too often, culture pressures us into thinking we need to produce "activity" that is not "in season" for us at the time. Then we judge ourselves by that inappropriate measuring stick. We need the voice of a successful farmer to help us understand where we are in "the process" and what activities we need to be involved in.

Remember the concentric cirlces? It's important for us to understand and embrace the "circle" we're in. Indifferent seasons there are different ways to live and different activities in which to be engaged.

Overall, what season do you feel like you are in right now, in reference to this metaphor of planting a garden? As a result, how then should you be living your life? Take a moment to write down your answer to these questions.

Your Next Four Action Steps:

Want to achieve results, solve your problems, and increase your happiness? There are actually four steps you can take to help in all those areas. They are:

1) **G**oals
2) **R**esponsibility
3) **O**bjective Thinking
4) **W**illingness

Let's take a closer look at each of these action steps:

Goals:

There's an ancient proverb that says,

"Without vision, people will perish!"

Ah! That's not good! Without a goal or planned destination, we're doomed to drift until, before long, drifting becomes the norm. When people ask how we're doing, we simply say, "Doin' good" or "Hangin' in there" or "Better 'n some."

But there's no reference point for us, and so the response is hollow.

Do you know what I mean? Have you ever said "Fine," but in your head you stop for a second and realize, *I'm not doing fine. But I don't want to get into it right now.*

People without destination tend to wander around a *lot*!

People without goals will always lower their daily expectations until just getting out of bed, going to work, just making enough money and waiting for the weekend becomes their definition of "I'm good."

That's the real danger of not having goals or a destination: *the status quo! Average!* Rather than breaking out of the status quo, we build a house and live there. Always wanting *more* but never quite grasping it!

However, for those that make the courageous decision to mark a destination, to stick a pin in the map of the future and declare, "This is where I'm going!" comes the remarkable treasure of *a vision, a hope, and a plan.* Until we mark a destination, we will never be sure which way to go or what decisions need to be made to get there. My dad used to say "Aim at nothing and you'll hit it every time!"

I remember working with a college graduate once, when I kind of absentmindedly helped him set some goals. Do you want to hear how it happened?

He had fallen for a cute little gal and was very interested in pursuing her as a girlfriend. So he gave me a call to ask my advice. I had been a sort of mentor to him for about five years so I was able to quickly size up the situation. He had *really slow* progress. I mean he was entrenched in some old thinking that he wasn't getting out of. Though he had graduated from college, he still lived at home, and had no job and no car! Now he wants to fall in love?

I knew this girls' father, so I already knew this relationship wasn't going anywhere if he stayed where he was. I told him, "John, here's the deal. You want to jump into a relationship but you have nothing to offer! You live at home, you have no car, and you have no job. If you asked my daughter out, *I'd* be showing up at the door! Before you start this thing, you need to at least have these three things taken care of."

In two weeks I got a text from him: "Guess who just got a car!"

Another couple of weeks, another text: "Just got an apartment with a buddy!"

After a couple more weeks: "Just landed a job at a college! I can't wait to call Amy!"

Whoa! The boy made more movement in two months than he had in the previous five years! Why? He just needed a worthy goal!

Unfortunately, I got a text a few days later… "Looks like the girlfriend thing is *not* going to happen!"

Responsibility: Owning vs. Blaming

Ah! I hated learning this lesson! Can you relate? It was so nice when I could just blame someone else for my problems! But unfortunately, blaming all those people for my problems never really helped my problems go away.

How about this phrase, "That's not fair!"

That thinking alone can wreck your life, because more often than not, "fair" is simply whatever we want it to be at the time. It's a more adult way of saying, "I want my way!"

When I blame, I give away my power to change to whatever I'm blaming! The weather, my spouse, my kids, the cops, my boss... blaming will always put me in The Victim Box! Can you relate?

However, when I begin to take responsibility for my own actions, then and only then will I position my thoughts to grow. Until this happens, I will always limit my growth to the boundaries of my comfort zone!

As soon as it becomes uncomfortable, I'll play the victim, give away my growth power, and shut down any forward movement. Someone who has taken personal responsibility recognizes an all-important truth about happiness: it depends much more on your attitude than it does on objective, external circumstances.

Remember the equation we discussed earlier:

$$A + B = C$$

My Situation + My interpretation = My response

C is related to B, not A! The variable is B not A! Your thinking is what changes, not just your circumstances. You must take responsibility for your interpretations!

Objective Thinking: Wisdom from a Mentor

You can only think what you think, and you can't think outside your box unless you have some help! That's the reason why you stare at the ceiling at night trying to figure out things and keep coming up with the same stuff!

This is what will continue to happen if you just keep trying to figure things out on your own.

I'm not saying this to condemn you—remember, this is the way we've all been programmed. The long and short of the truth is this:

You can't change yourself by yourself!

However, if we could be open to raising our hands and asking questions and bringing mentors into our lives, questions can actually have answers! And then we could get some sleep!

The bottom line for personal or professional mentoring is that it achieves a great deal of change. We don't even need the stats to prove to us the value of mentorship! It's a no-brainer... and yet so few people do it!

Who do you have to help you with your objective thinking?

Willingness: Learn and Change

Okay, now you have the right goals in place, you've decided to take responsibility for your own destiny and actions, and you've decided to raise your hand and get qualified help. Now all that's missing is...

Doing!

The question is:

Are you willing to do the work?

Here's another equation for you:

Learn + Change = Growth!

In other words, in non-mathematic terms, willingness is the *ultimate accelerator* for growth.

Are you teachable? Are you willing to admit when you need help? It took me a *long* time to get to this place. I wanted different results but I wasn't willing to ask for help to think outside my box and make changes.

I just kept getting the same results! I wasn't willing to raise my hand and discover what I didn't know!

Your growth is only limited by your willingness to embrace learning and changing.

However, if you can find the courage to say *yes*, the world opens up! New options enter into the equation and your mind begins to change!

Growth is a choice—are you willing to choose?

It's not about ability; it's simply a question of *willingness.*

Are you willing to go on the journey to discover yourself?

Because when we truly discover ourselves, we automatically realize how much we need others!

Do you want to grow? Do you feel like its time for a shift, a transformation into something new, something better, something more? Are you willing to create space in your life to allow this new growth to happen?

All the principles you've learned in this book apply, whether you want personal growth or professional growth. Use them. Contact me and let's have coffee!

Your growth is the most important thing in your life!

You were made for something big!

You were designed to have massive impact on this earth!

Don't settle for anything less than the dream you have for your ultimate design!

Appendix A

The Seven Keys to Living in Balance

So, are you busy? Crazy-busy? Have you ever felt at one time or another that your life was simply out of balance? Like there was just way too much of one thing and not enough of the other? What do you think people conclude when they are in this position? Would you like to feel in balance?

Here are just a few external pressures we might have to deal with:

- Marriage
- Work
- Health
- Time
- Money

What do you have inside of you to balance out these external pressures? How can you develop an internal push back or resolve that will keep you from getting knocked off course or squeezed to death by all the external pressures?

Balance doesn't necessarily come just from leaving one thing so you can do another. That could actually lead to imbalance in the other direction. No, the answer is to be able to do *both* on a daily basis... internal and external!

Let's talk about seven keys to get BALANCE, which are...

- B: Believe
- A: Allow
- L: Lifelong Learning
- A: Allegiance

- N: "No!"
- C: Care
- E: Expression

Let's look at those individually now:

Believe

Believe there's something more, something to counter the weight of work!

Have you given up? Is it possible there's more to life than what you are currently experiencing? Have you settled into a way of thinking which says, "This is just how it is and I better just get used to it"?

Without belief that things could be different, you can easily fall into the trap of settling for the status quo. Many people do! They get into the flow of "daily management" of their lives and forget they were actually moving towards something before they got hypnotized by the phrase "I'm fine."

After 15 years of teaching school and gaining "security" in the form of salary, tenure, retirement, benefits, etc., I made a leap to corporate leadership (I was 37 years old!).

After 10 years of C-level leadership with established salary, benefits, and a good reputation with the company, I made another leap! I believed there was more for me to do! Not that teaching or C-level leadership were wrong or beneath me. I simply believed there was more for me to do, to experience.

So I made the leap, because I didn't feel like I could continue to grow into my full design while remaining in those positions. (I was 47 years old!)

I felt I had reached a ceiling and didn't want to get stuck at that level of impacting the earth. I wanted more, and I *believed* there was more!

Take a moment to think of an area where you may have slipped into thinking, *I just better get used to this.* Work? Family? Marriage?

Friends? Finances? How has that thinking affected your energy and performance?

Write it down!

ALLOW

Allow for open space and time in your schedule. Look at these sobering statistics regarding just those in the workplace:

- 67% of employees surveyed feel they have no time for their kids.
- 63% of employees surveyed feel they have no time for their spouse.
- 55% of employees surveyed feel they have no time for themselves.
- "I just don't have enough time right now!" This is the ultimate killer of dreams! "I'll just have to get to it later!" This is called procrastination and it will *always* lead to a broken heart. At best it produces differed success; at worst it produces hollow hopes because it lacks deliberate follow-through.

Growth takes time and space; it must be free from distractions. I'm not saying your job is a distraction, but if we're not intentional about remaining on the growth path, then our job, family, entertainment, and countless other things can become distractions that keep us from achieving our full impact on the earth. Not just some impact—our full impact!

When planting, you have to clear a space first and prepare the ground for new ideas and new activities. No space, no growth!

"I just don't have enough time!" This consistent mentality will inhibit growth and balance in your life. You *must be deliberate with your time!* I guarantee that if you don't intentionally fill it, external forces will take over! It's not that they're all bad. You just want to make sure they are external forces you have deliberately chosen!

I find this often with my corporate clients who come to me desiring change in their organization. They feel out of control. They cry out for change, but as we begin to walk through the steps for automatic growth,

I often find that they haven't taken the time to implement the steps! It's not that they refuse to do them, they just can't seem to make them *fit* amidst all the chaos they are trying to maintain so they can keep their company in the black!

Can you think of one or two times where you have desired to see growth, but you didn't provide the space for it to happen? Maybe you could revisit that desire and this time commit to creating space for it?

Write it down!

LIFELONG LEARNING

Positive growth requires both experiential knowledge and emotional processing. This is the kind of knowledge you gain through experience, as well as the kind of emotional processing which helps you implement that new knowledge into your life.

It's important to note that this is ongoing learning that goes *beyond* your professional development. When was the last time your read a book for pleasure? Did you even finish it? How long did it take?

When was the last time you read a book on personal growth? Did you learn? Were you challenged? Did you experience a pressure as you encounter new ways of thinking that conflicted with the old? How did you process this pressure?

When was the last time you had an outdoor adventure? (Scraping ice off your windshield doesn't count)

Here are three steps to becoming a successful life long learner!

1) *Obtaining New Information.* This is vital! This could be new information about an old problem or simply about a desired topic. Contrary to popular belief, you *can't* grow just by recycling your old mindset! Remember: most people's big picture about life was formed by what they learned by the age of thirteen! Stretching experiences are the best tool to use for learning new things.

2) *Interpretation.* Just because we read a new book doesn't necessarily mean it will impact the way we think. Information alone won't bring about personal growth—we must learn how to interpret what we learn. Information with the wrong interpretation can lead to disaster! Who is helping you interpret your new information?

3) *Application.* This is the final critical step in learning. You may have learned the right thing and interpreted it rightly, but if you misapply it, it could lead to some poor outcomes.

You can only think what you think! It's impossible for you think anything but what you think. The only way for us to think new thoughts is if we allow an *outside source influence* our thinking. So, what outside sources are you intentionally allowing to influence your life? Media? Friends? Culture? Work? Mentors? This is where I put in a strong word of encouragement for mentors in your life *and to be a mentor to someone else*! Also, be sure to journal.

Take a second to think of something that you would like to learn about that has nothing to do with your job. Do you think you could take some steps this week to begin that learning process? Who is helping you interpret and apply your new information?

Write it down!

ALLEGIANCE

You must retain allegiance to your core *personal* purpose, not just your professional purpose.

This connects to a belief that you have a core purpose on this earth which goes beyond making enough money to provide for a specific lifestyle for you and your family. That's wonderful to do, but that in itself will not be enough to bring fulfillment over the long haul. It may work in the short term, but we all know the feeling of working hard for our money and getting the paycheck and wondering, *Is this all there is to my life?*

Knowing your core purpose allows you to make decisions along the way. If we don't know our identity, then we'll always be up for interpretation by work, culture, people, and pressures. We'll try to be something we feel *pressured* to be rather than to grow into the person we truly are with all our gifts and talents to offer our work and our community.

Once this core purpose is understood, you have to fight for it! Almost daily, your core purpose will be attacked by the urgent management of that day's to-do list! This doesn't mean to-do lists are wrong or bad (in fact, they're very important), you just want to make sure the things on the list are getting you where you want to go!

Have you gotten through a very busy day, then looked back at the end of it and felt like you accomplished very little? This is probably unavoidable at times, but you don't want to make a habit out of it.

Aim for a target *of your choosing*! The alternative is to aim for a target someone else has determined for you (feeling out of control) or to aim at nothing (feeling lost or stuck).

Take a second to consider one of your core purposes. What activity gives you life and energy? What is something you could do for five hours straight and still have energy to keep going? That's probably one of your core identities!

Here's a glimpse at my core purposes to get you started. When I am doing these activities, I feel like I am fulfilling my purpose on earth:

- Affect change
- Empower and equip people
- Speak and teach
- Connect and network

My friend who's a chemical engineer got moved into a managerial position at his company because he did such a great job in the lab! Bad idea! Engineers aren't always known for their social skills. He didn't just get a promotion—he also got depression, anxiety, sleep disorders, high blood pressure, and poor blood chemistry! He took the job because of the pay, without considering his *core purpose!*

Consider your core purpose.

Write it down!

"No!"

You need to learn how and when to say no!

This connects directly to maintaining allegiance to your core purpose. The goal isn't to say "No" to more things—it's to say "No" to the things that don't move you forward in your personal growth and development. If you cannot be effective, or if something will drain the resources of your time, treasure, and talent, then you need to say "No!"

Most of us bend to external pressures and say "Yes" out of a sense of obligation. If you lack an internal core purpose of identity, then you're probably doomed to being controlled by this pressure on in to the future.

So when do you say "No?" It's determined by your core identity!

When I am asked to do something that doesn't allow me to do one or more of my core purposes, I will probably say "No." This applies to taking a job, making a move, starting a venture, or accepting an invitation to be a part of something in my community or in my church. If it will allow me to do one or more of the four core things I outlined above, then I will probably love doing it and not feel drained. Instead, I'm more inclined to say "Yes," and be of much better service because I'm working in my *core!*

Take a quick moment to think of one or two areas where you probably need to say "No." Now simply develop an exit strategy over the next 2-4 weeks. *Get in balance!*

Write it down!

Care

Care for and serve others.

If all my time is filled with myself, I guarantee I will not find the balance I seek! A key ingredient for balance is *caring for and giving to others*. Voluntarily giving of yourself to benefit someone else! Like saying "No," you can't be pressured into caring for others and receive the benefit of *balance*. This has to altruistic. (And it doesn't necessarily include running your kids all over town to soccer practice!)

I would strongly recommend you decide on just *one* area to care for others outside of your own home, then set a goal of remaining consistent with it. Caring for others allows us to keep the Big Picture in sight—if we just continually focus on ourselves and our agendas, we can easily slip into a narrow-mindedness that will continue to knock us out of balance.

In fact, many times when I come to the conclusion that all I need is a good vacation—time to get away and spend on me—I have found that a couple of hours spent selflessly caring for and meeting the needs of someone else give me the refreshing perspective I so desperately needed. Coaching a team, volunteering at your kids school, feeding the homeless, collecting food or clothing for the less fortunate, mentoring a younger person in their personal growth… anything you can find where you are using your time, talent, treasure, or touch to benefit someone else's life is a key ingredient for *balance*.

Take a quick moment to think of one or two areas where you can implement this into your life. My wife and I teach the college and career group at our church and have them over for dinner at our house one night a week (it fits one of our core purposes to speak and teach).

Can you think of an opportunity within your sphere of influence right now where you could step in and help someone else on a consistent basis? I encourage you to take steps this week to position yourself to fill that need!

Write it down!

EXPRESSION

You must find an expression for your passions outside of work.

The final key ingredient to find and maintain balance in your life is to have opportunities to express your passions! Art, cars, sports, writing, dance, playing an instrument... there are a ton of passions out there—the question is: which ones are yours?

It's not uncommon for me to work with a life-coaching client who is depressed and lost and cannot come up with an answer for the question, "What are you passionate about?" Obviously, I'm talking about healthy passions here! "I love beer!" should not be a passion on this list! Slow down, Sparky!

If you are not allowing space in your life to engage in what ignites your passion, then you can easily find yourself cold and emotionless, like a candle that has been blown out.

I once had a client who had a passion for shapes and angles. No kidding! He would spend hours drawing designs on grid paper made up completely of straight lines. Not a single arc on the page! He even framed them and gave them as gifts. I never really understood it, but he loved it! He had a passion, so he included this expression in his life.

This expression must come out from within you! It can't just be going along with a group. It must be *your* passion and it must be *expressed*!

So, what are you passionate about? Do you think it's possible to take steps this week to include some expression of that passion? What would that look like?

Write it down!

APPENDIX B

BECOMING IMMORTAL –
THE POWER OF JOURNALING

Journaling—the act of writing down your thoughts and ideas on a regular basis—has many, many benefits. Here are just a few *scientific* benefits:

- Improve your physical and mental wellness
- Decrease symptoms of depression, panic, anxiety, substance abuse, PTSD, asthma, arthritis, and many other negative health conditions and disorders
- Expand your ability to process and problem solve
- Make therapy sessions more effective
- Strengthen your immune system and prevent a host of illnesses
- Counteract the negative effects of stress

Beyond these scientific benefits, as well as helping you articulate yourself and reflect on your inner feelings and ideas, journaling also offers many *practical* benefits as well. Benefits like:

Never forgetting anything.

It's often not long before we forget about memorable times and experiences we've had. The feelings and memories begin to fade as time goes by, until eventually you may forget about the experience altogether. A diary or a personal journal is a great way to keep your memory in line.

Improving your writing skills.

Writing everyday isn't just a pointless chore—it helps you become a better writer for multiple endeavors. If you have a job where articulating yourself in written form is important, pick up a pen and start journaling today!

Discovering and knowing yourself.

Ever wonder exactly how your own mind works? Ever sifted through the events of the day and looked at the way you really felt about a situation? Sometimes our thoughts are so clouded with the hectic this-and-that of everyday that we don't get a chance to pinpoint our own feelings! Writing it out is often the only way to really know yourself.

Spiritual development.

This carries on from the last point. Knowing yourself helps you get in touch with your spiritual side. Like a form of meditation, journaling helps promote mindfulness and awareness of your actions and thoughts.

Goal setting.

We often don't know exactly what we want out of our days, weeks, or even life as a whole. Keeping a journal can help you sort out your goals and set tangible targets. Try this out the next time you pick up the pen.

Inspiration and Motivation

Use your journal as motivation to reach your goals! Keeping yourself accountable for those goals and constantly reminding yourself of them will keep you focused on the prize.

Stay organized.

Our thoughts and ideas can be a jumbled mess without some sort of order. Writing things out—or mind-mapping them—breaks that jumble down into workable pieces. If you journal electronically (i.e. on your computer, tablet, smartphone, or private blog) it's even easier, as you can tag entries and search for key terms.

Vent your emotions

Get things off your chest! Bottling up your negative emotions breeds more negativity, and a journal is safe place to release them with no repercussions or hurt feelings. Let 'em out!

Get creative.

Writing daily is bound to spark a flame of creativity in your soul. Try adding emotional sketches to further fuel that creativity .

Live a more interesting life.

You must have *something* to write about everyday, right? The accountability of a journal forces you to seek adventure (or see the adventure that's been in front of you all along).

GOING BEYOND "SCIENTIFIC BENEFITS"

So those are some of the scientific and practical benefits of journaling, all of which are true, but hardly any of which is very *inspiring*. Putting your focus solely on the benefits of journaling takes the activity to a clinical, objective level that robs it of its beauty.

To truly enjoy journaling, we must look beyond benefits.

Did you see the movie *Dead Poets Society*? Remember the first day that John Keating, Robin Williams's character, came into class and asks a student to read the introduction to their poetry book written by "Mr. J. Evans Pritchard." There's all this talk about measurement and numbers and graphs and outcomes, and at the end, Keating replies, "Excrement!" He commands all his students to rip the introduction out of the book! "I don't hear any ripping!" Oh, being a classroom teacher for fifteen years, I was always inspired by that movie and how Professor Keating encouraged new thinking!

After having all his students remove the offensive introductions to their books of poetry, John Keating says, "We don't read and write poetry because it's cute. We read and write poetry because we are members of the human race. And the human race is filled with passion. Medicine, law, business, engineering, these are noble pursuits and necessary to *sustain life*. But poetry, beauty, romance, love, these are *what we stay alive for*."

Each of these benefits of journaling is very true and very real—but we do not write because of the *outcomes*, we write because of what *comes out*!

I've been journaling since 1988. Up until that time I had tried to start journaling several times with a lot of starts and stops. I would always use my journal to keep notes from teachings I had heard or keep a list of things to do. Eventually, my desire to write all this down would fade, because I mainly just viewed it as a way to keep track of information and I felt like I could just do that in my head. So... why write?

However, in 1988, I entered into a major transition in my life and felt compelled to chronicle the story as it played out. Remember how I hid in the closet after college graduation because I was scared to enter the open seas of the marketplace? Well, in 1988 I left that citadel of security and moved to Plymouth, Massachusetts to live with my sister and brother-in-law and take time to figure out my life. (It was an amazing time filled with tremendous growth for me, but that's another story for another book.)

So there I was, traveling halfway across the United States on I-40 between Oklahoma City and Memphis in my little Honda Accord and I started thinking, *Wow, this is huge! What the heck am I doing? I think I'm starting a Vision Quest!* And I knew I needed to keep track of the experience. So I stopped in Memphis and picked up the first journal I ever completed! It was just a little black sketchbook, hardcover, with unlined blank pages. I loved it! I also bought a brand-new, black ink pen to complete the toolkit.

About a week after I arrived in Plymouth (which, coincidentally, was part of the Vision Quest of the Pilgrims), I settled in to engaging with my journal to log the events of my journey.

November 5, 1988

This is my first entry into this new journal. I've put it off for several days because it intimidated me. I felt that I had to have real serious thoughts full of deep meaning before I could write them down. I guess I still feel that way to some degree. I've always wanted to keep a daily journal. It makes me feel important. Now as I look back, it would be fascinating to be able to find out what was going through my head one, two, or even six years ago. Hopefully in six years I'll be able to return to these pages and discover in them my growth emotionally, spiritually and even physically. If nothing else, I've already learned one thing already from writing in this journal … THIS PEN LEAKS THROUGH THE PAGE!!

The reason why I have exclusively chosen now to begin this jour-nal is because I have just made a BIG move in my life. I no longer live in Oklahoma. I have entered a new adventure in New England. My move to Plymouth, Massachusetts came at a time when I needed to get away for a while. My involvement in youth ministry had become more of a job or a task than what I believe it was conceived to be or supposed to be.

Man, even now as I think back, there seems to be so much I need to write down about the past few years, simply so I will fully understand what I am thinking when I read this in the future.

I suppose, to quickly sum up, I should say that I was so involved with MY world, my time, my schedule, my job, my needs, my wants, my bubble, that I couldn't see out to others and feel their hurts or their troubles. By focus-ing so much on ME, I had lost my way.

So now I'm here in Plymouth to regroup and hopefully receive new vision for the future. My hope for this journal is that it can be uniquely mine and that I'll be able to write things in it that may be difficult to say out loud. We'll see how it goes. I feel better now that I have written some. I think I'm gonna like this!"

That was my first entry in Book #1. I was 24 years old.

And now here I am, 25 years later as of right now, just finishing up my 35th little black sketchbook. It's weird how my journal has become so close to me, even an extension of me. Even though I have 35 different books, I refer to all of them as if they were one—my journal—because it's one continual story that follows me through all the events and experi-ences (good and bad) of my adult life. I spent two years in Plymouth and they were everything I had anticipated. During those two years, my life was radically changed—and much of it was extremely painful. But that is even another story.

Oh, and I still buy a new pen with every new journal.

Well, how about you? What are you thoughts on journaling? Are you like I was? Do you have a drawer or a shelf filled with partially-completed journals? If you do, don't throw those away. They will become very valuable to you (and others) in the future.

WHAT I'VE LEARNED ABOUT JOURNALING

Over the past years, I've learned a few things about journaling (or maybe what journaling has taught me)…

1) *Don't worry about the back story!* If it's been a long time, don't feel like you have to catch up—this kills the process. I've had times when it may have been a month or so since I had written. Then I would finally sit down and it would take me a hour just to get caught up, but by that time, I would be worn out and not want to write anymore—and I hadn't even gotten to what I wanted to write about! Ah! Don't get caught in this trap. I promise, you'll remember the back story without writing down what you missed.

2) *Write for YOU!* The power of the journal is when you write to *yourself* and no one else. This is what usually pressured me into thinking I had to fill in the back story or have all the answers to any questions I wrote down. I felt like if someone were to read this, it would need to make sense to them, so it should follow a smooth order where one thing would lead to another. That's a classic, process-killing trap! You're not writing a screenplay here (although you may in the future based on your journal), so don't worry about all the flow. Write to *you!* You'll understand it because it's you! It's not a book; it's your life!

3) *It will come in cycles.* You can't force journaling—it needs to be natural or else it will quickly be shoved to the side. Many times

a lack of something to write about is either caused by a *huge* distraction (pain, love, or busy-ness) or it's due to a lack of engagement in life. I've had each of these distractions and, for a time, just didn't have time to write. I've also had seasons where I just stopped engaging in life, checking out and robotically moving through my days. I'm sure you've never done this, but you may know someone who has. Soon, days became weeks and, well, you know the story. Your journal encourages you to engage and interact with your life.

4) *It's a risk.* Yes, it is possible someone will read it! Don't let this stop you. My wife read my journal once while we were dating. She got upset and angry and wanted to argue with me until I said, "That's my journal—it's not a letter." She hasn't read it since… that I know of! Your journal is made up of all the stuff that flies through your head and heart, and just because you think something, that doesn't mean it's *who you are*; and just because you felt something yesterday, that doesn't mean you feel it today. Each of us is in constant flux. It would be unfortunate to limit what you write and process simply because you were afraid of someone reading it. Now, it's possible to have some trust issues going on with people around you, and if that the case, find a safe place for your journal where people (younger siblings, snoopy friends, etc.) won't find it. (Though the fact that you have to hide it may be an indicator of something you should look into.) When you write it, you own it. Sometimes I didn't want to own what I was writing. I didn't want that to be me, and I surely didn't want anyone else to know that about me. So, I felt a need to hide it. Well, I got over that and you will too.

5) *Connect rewards to writing.* New pens, coffee, music, comfortable chairs, solitude, warm blankets, outside, awesome views, bookstores, coffee shops… these are all rewards I connect to journaling. Having these places and props cause me to get

excited about writing. I remember one time passing through Niagara Falls, New York and I couldn't wait to wake up at sunrise, get on my mountain bike and ride to the Falls and write in my journal while listening to the soundtrack to the film *The Mission*! It was awesome! If I feel like writing is going to be a chore, I probably won't do it. But if I connect that journal time to allowing myself a moment to sit in an overstuffed leather chair in a coffee shop or bookstore while drinking from an oversized mug of legal stimulants, I will make sure it becomes part of my day or week. Just connect a reward you would really enjoy and it can change your whole attitude.

6) *Let it out!* Write with the intent of getting something out of you and onto paper. If you don't have anything wanting out, then maybe you don't have to write. If you mostly write when there's nothing to write, it will become mundane and lose value… and if it loses value, you'll stop doing it. Sometimes, there's just nothing to say. Some people have nothing to say! I think those of us who have nothing to say are simply too busy doing and haven't taken the time to just *be*. As a result, all we know to talk about is our work or what's in the news.

7) *Don't sweat the grammar.* Let it flow! If you decide to write a book using your journals, you can correct the grammar at that time. But don't worry about it while you're writing. Remember, this isn't a book—it's your life!

8) *Leave Dr. Phil out of it.* Don't put the pressure on yourself to have all the answers. This goes back to not worrying about back story. It's so easy to fall into a trap of putting some kind of understandable structure to your writing: "Here's what's going on. Here's why it's going on. Here's what I need to do to increase/decrease what's going on. Here's what I did. Here's how it turned out." Yeah, good luck with that! In the long run, you'll discover your growth in maturity will be

measured more by the *questions you ask* than the *answers you have.*

I'm sure there are many other things I've learned from journaling, but what *I* have learned isn't what's important here—this is about what *you* will learn! And although you may have similar revelations as I did, you will also have a whole host of other lessons to glean from and feed to others!

If you're new to journaling, let me take just a few lines and put some structure to what you're supposed to write. As I've said before, you can write anything you want, but sometimes that can be a little overwhelming to the new writer, like a painter being confronted with a life-size blank canvas armed with only a small palette of paint in his hand. So, let me give you some numbers to paint by as you begin. Over time you will no longer need them and probably even come to view them as restraining.

So, you have gone out and bought a journal and a brand new pen to go along with it. You're now sitting in an overstuffed chair in the back corner of a used bookstore that smells of dust and old leather. You open your journal for the first time and hear the spine cracking as it reluctantly reveals the treasure it's been successfully protecting until now—the first blank page!

Ahhh!

Don't freak out. Here are some suggestions to help you begin filling up those pages. These suggestions start with what I hope will be very basic information that provides the least amount of intimidation before gradually moving into deeper and deeper levels of self-awareness. Find a level you're comfortable with and stay there for a while. You don't have to start out by swimming in the deep end of the pool!

1) **Data**—Start with simple data; just information like the time, temperature, a description of the room you're in, the clothes you're wearing, the events going on in your life, people who are influencing you and so on. I do this on every new entry

in my journal. In the upper left corner I write the time, the date, where I am, the temperature outside, and something about the weather. I'm always surprised at how easy it is to go back to those pages years later and be able to remember those exact details! This is great stuff to write when you're on a trip or vacation, or are doing something out of the norm.

2) **Effects of the Data**—What is happening because of these activities or events or people? You may keep this at a purely physical level or you may go a little deeper and talk about how these events and people are affecting you personally. Keep it in third person if you want, and talk about how you see other people being affected (good or bad). What types of actions are you or others taking or wanting to take based upon the situation?

3) **Questions about the Data**—Why is this happening? What did that mean? What should I do? Don't worry about the answers just yet. Simply keep track of all your questions. Remember, your ultimate growth will be measured by the questions you ask, not the answers you have. This is a deeper level and requires a little more interaction with your surroundings. Archie Bunker, for those of you old enough to remember, never went to this level! He just saw in two dimensions. He would see and he would interpret, and most of his interpretations led him to interpret that everyone else on earth was an idiot!

4) **Statements of Value**—This is when you begin to engage in the process of discovering *why* you believe what you believe, when you start digging in to your conclusions and discovering the beliefs leading you to those conclusions. *"This is what's going on. This is how it's affecting me. It raises these questions in me. And these are my answers and conclusions to those questions. Why am I coming to this conclusion? Are my conclusions appropriate in this situation or for this time in my life?"* This discovery isn't always easy and most of the time will require an objective point of view

to help you see it. Left to ourselves, we will continually come to the same conclusions: "Everyone else on earth is an idiot." You will need a trusted influencer in your life to help you see past your conclusions and into your belief system. (See chapter five for a fuller discussion on the importance of a mentor.)

5) **Feelings (Emotions)**—This is usually the reason people don't want to journal to begin with—they don't want to "get in touch with their feelings." I was asked that one time by a person who was pushing just a little too hard on me—"Clay, what are you feeling?" they asked. "I'm feeling angry and like I want to punch you!" came my reply. Well remember, this is *way* down on the list of things to write about in your journal, so don't let this vulnerable, touchy-feely stuff intimidate you. You don't have to go here if you aren't ready.

6) **Thoughts and Fears**—This level can take a while to get to, and you'll definitely want to have a mentor or an influencer in your life help you navigate these deep waters. Most people walking around today are controlled by their fears. It's not always a bad thing, but it can eventually erode your perspective on life and cause you to come to consistently negative conclusions, which become the engine for all your decisions and actions even towards people you love. How you think is the most important thing about you. Using your journal to dig down to this depth of self-evaluation can truly transform you into a new person—and that person may be the person you have always *felt* you were, but never could connect to. Few people are able to tap into this level of self-awareness; I have found journaling to be a wonderful tool to aid in the process.

As you move from level 1 to level 6, you may recognize the process of TFBAR! Levels one and two mainly address the external *results and actions* of yourself and others. Levels three and four move deeper into the *beliefs and feelings* we act upon. And levels five and six tap in to the very core of who we are… How we *think*!

Our thoughts will always determine our feelings.

Our feelings shape our beliefs.

Our beliefs motivate our actions.

Our actions produce the results we experience in our lives.

So how you think is the most important thing about you! At it's very best, journaling helps you get in touch with how you *think*!

Appendix C

Write Your Story
(The Results of the Sticky
Note Timeline)

In late September of 2009, after eight years of being out of the classroom, I suddenly became excited about getting back. I didn't understand the sudden change. If you had asked me the day before if I would ever go back to classroom teaching, I would have said, "No, why would I ever do that?"

And yet, here I was with a burning desire to be back in the classroom.

The timing of this desire was really poor. It was late September, and school had already started. If I had only known this was going to happen a few months earlier I would have had a much better chance of actually finding a position! But, there I was—school had started and I was late to class.

My motivation? Money.

My family's financial situation was pretty bleak then, with little hope for future change (you know that place?), and the income and benefits provided by a teaching position would help a lot. After receiving permission from my wife (another amazing story), I began to put out feelers looking for any schools that may be realizing they made a hiring mistake with a science teacher after seeing them in class for two months. Yes, I knew my chances were slim! But after a few weeks I received a call from my sister saying there was a private, Catholic school looking for a science teacher for the second semester! Boom! The plan was coming together!

I ended up getting that position and launched into a season of working two full-time jobs. It was a wonderful experience that became strategic for my overall journey, but after three semesters, as you can imagine, I was tired! I enjoyed both jobs, but was caught in a tug-of-war between which direction to pursue. I viewed my choices as either choosing a job I was passionate about but that didn't provide the needed revenue or the job that provided a pretty good revenue but didn't light me up. It was tough! My blood pressure was going up and I wasn't sleeping well. I even feel like I has slipped into the beginnings of a depression.

It was about this time, spring of 2010, that a good friend of mine, Danny Kittinger, introduced me to a man named Dave Jewitt. Dave spends his days helping men navigate their lives towards their true identity, or "design," to use his words.

Dave and I met over coffee, and it didn't take much time explaining my position before I was crying and hiding my face from the other coffee drinkers. I was simply at the end of my strength! I didn't understand where I was in my life story; I was extremely busy, but felt like I was on a treadmill going nowhere! I felt like I had missed something—some turn in my life that had sent me on a wild goose chase for too many years!

While I sat there blubbering, Dave gently replied, "So you're, what, mid-forties?"

"Yes," I responded.

"Well, Clay," Dave said, "you're right on track! You're right where you need to be." I didn't know if I should believe him, but, wow, it was so encouraging! (More tissues, please!)

Dave went on to explain the life stages everyone goes through, from your learning years to your investing years. He also asked me several questions about other thoughts and emotions I was experiencing.

"How did you know I was thinking and feeling these things?" I asked.

"Your questions and emotions are very typical for the stage of life you're in," he said. "You're right where you should be." What a wonderful relief!

We went on to spend the next few months meeting, with Dave helping me discover my true design through mapping my own story and looking at the big picture.

So now I want to share with you what my path looks like and what I have *learned to learn* from it. I'm not doing this because my story is anything out of the ordinary—I'm doing it because I want to use my story as a template to help you map *yours*! This was a powerful exercise for me and it helped me discover, not only *who* I am (an elementary discovery foundational to all long-term, healthy growth) but also *why* I am and *how* I got this way!

Once I had a better understanding of the path I was on, it wasn't very hard at all to determine my next steps. It's really that simple! Your true identity will always provide you with a clear course of action! However, most of us get this backwards and try to use a specific course of action to lead us to our identity. This is why so many of us find our identity in what we *do*, in our job or our responsibility in life. What's that quote by Henry Thoreau? "Most men live lives of quiet desperation." I think he was alluding to this trap.

I'll keep this brief because it's not so much my story itself I want you to hear as much as how to process your own story. So, lets take a walk together...

THE LEARNING YEARS

We'll call the time between birth and age thirteen the Learning Years. If you were to sum up in one word the major lesson I learned during this time, it would probably be *Leader*. I grew up in a Christian family with demonstrative extroverts for parents. Trying to get a word in around our dinner table took a lot of self-confidence and a loud voice to break in to the five other loud conversations going on—especially when you're the youngest.

It was during these years I learned that family is always there (our family of six lived in a 980-square-foot mobile home for eleven years—they were *always* there!). I also learned that I liked popularity and the way it could get you things. I learned that reputation was important along with winning, being funny, and working together on a team. I also developed my concepts of friendship, loyalty, and relationships at this young age. These are just some of the foundations I formed during these Learning Years, when , I came to believe…

- I am talented
- Talent gets attention
- Attention means acceptance
- Acceptance means security

I also believed in *me*! I can do it! I know the answer! I'm in control, and I like it! Leaders got to be in control so I liked leadership!

Now I know my parents and other teachers were not the source of all I learned! In fact, in some instances I'm sure they were actually trying to teach me the very opposite. But this is how my little pea brain interpreted all those early experiences: life, pretty much, revolved around me—and I liked it that way!

I also picked up a lot of skills and competencies during my Learning Years; skills I would use and eventually make money with in my future. Skills like leadership, speaking in front of crowds, how to light a pilot light, how to mow the lawn, athletics, a sense of humor, competitiveness, sarcasm, and manipulation, among many others.

These were *my* early Learning Years. How about yours? What did you learn—good or bad?

1. What significant events happened in your life in your Learning Years?
2. Who were the significant people in your life in your Learning Years?
3. What did you come to believe about yourself through these experiences and relationships?

4. What specific skills did you learn?
5. What beliefs did you adopt about yourself, authority, God, justice, trust, relationships? There may be many other beliefs that you're able to identify as well.

Please take the time to write this stuff down. You may want to just read on and get to the answer, but you must remember: *the answer lies within you*! You have to dig, explore, and process to discover *your* map! My map won't work for you—there may be some similarities, but your map is specific to you. So, take some time to walk through each of these questions for each stage of your life, however long it may have lasted.

THE BUILDING YEARS

Based upon our early conclusions, we begin to build our lives, moving forward with new experiences and new relationships. Life happens to us and we interpret the events according to our conclusions and our definitions of what is true and just and right. We usually don't stop to consider our definitions; we simply make assumptions about life so our definitions will hold up.

As a result, many times during our teens and twenties, we tend to see the reasons for our struggles as coming from some external force—

- "It's because of my parents that…"
- "My girlfriend/boyfriend made me…"
- "I can't believe my boss…"

Because we rarely stop to consider the validity of our preconceived conclusions, we rarely take responsibility for our actions when negative things happen. (Back when I was a teacher, when students made As, they assumed it was because of their great effort—when they made Ds, it naturally became *my* fault!)

My Building Years happened between the ages of 14 and 18. You may have a different title and time frame, but this is how my map lays out. It's when I started making more of my own decisions based upon what *I* wanted to do rather than just waking up and moving from place to place as my mom and dad ordered.

For the most part, this made up my junior high and high school years. Wow, no wonder these years are so chaotic for kids—they're all trying to force life to fit their conclusions! This makes things very emotional and volatile. No one seems to do what you want him or her to do for any length of time and it causes you to feel like your world is going to shatter! It's a constant struggle to get everything and everyone to line up with your demands so you can feel like life is okay. Then someone messes it up and the house of cards comes crumbling down again.

(I taught junior high for three years. Wow! During that time I wasn't the kind and understanding person I am today - ha! - and would feel totally drained at the end of each day because I was still trying to do the same thing! At 26, I was still trying to line everyone and everything up with what I wanted so I could feel okay. And, let me tell you, leaning on a junior high student to make you feel okay is *not* a good idea!)

My high school days were really wonderful. I used the skills I had gained when I was younger to excel in athletics and used my leadership skills to become an influencer. Popularity was important, so I made sure I was noticed (much to my teachers' chagrin). I could sing, so I was in the musical. I could manipulate teachers so I didn't have to study much. I was considerate (sometimes) and agreeable, so I got along with most everyone.

It was working out. Yes, I had struggles, but that was just because other people were stupid and didn't know that I knew better. I got along with my parents because I didn't give them any strong reasons to lay down the law. I was a good student and was always involved in some organized sport, so I was rarely out late. Plus, I had a steady girlfriend, so they always knew where I was!

My personality and talent were strong enough and my home life stable enough that I was able to walk through these years with relative ease—further validating all my conclusions and leading me to believe I really had figured it all out!

And I wasn't even out of my teens!

What about your Building Years?

1. When did they occur?
2. What skills did you learn?
3. Which skills served you well?
4. Which ones should you have left by the wayside?

Write down the answers to these questions and any others that might arise as a result of your Building Years.

THE TESTING YEARS

You may have experienced this stage as well, when you begin to discover that your conclusions don't really work anymore and the wheels of life are starting to come off. My Testing Years happened between the ages of 18 and 31. I had become very comfortable being a leader and feeling the security of being in control. I thought life would be like that forever—just expanding my ability to control more and more things. It would just be a matter of me applying my formula (conclusions) to a broader and broader sphere as I grew older. Well, I came to discover that wasn't really how life worked!

My Testing Years started when a series of events in college shook my foundation. My girlfriend of five years broke up with me, I quit playing football and had to change my major because I was flunking all my classes! Although I was still using my skills I had learned in my earlier stages, these skills weren't producing the outcomes they once had.

I was so angry! Other people were letting me down! For the first time in my life, I wasn't able to control them and make them do what I wanted! This didn't fit!

By the time I graduated, I had lost a lot of confidence in my ability to control life and became very afraid I wasn't ready for the next step. In other words, I was scared to death of what I was going to do next! So, out of fear, I fell back on what I had found success with in earlier years—working with kids as a youth leader in a church. I'm not saying that being a youth leader is a bad thing; it's just that I was doing it because I was afraid of moving forward. I found something I knew I could do and held on to it for safety.

Over the next several years, most of the other conclusions I leaned on to feel security were tested and shattered as well. I made some poor decisions that cut me off from my relationship with my family, one of which led to me being fired by my dad from the family business, where I anticipated spending most of my working years.

I spent two years losing every competition I was involved in, literally going 0-30 on two different men's basketball teams while the first high school football team I coached went 0-10! Painful! I could no longer rely on my ability to win and compete to find security!

I became very isolated from all my friends, traded my sense of humor for a sharp cynicism, financial failure constantly nipped at my heels, and then I experienced a failed marriage, leaving me feeling a loneliness I never knew existed. (This is what led me to the closet at the beginning of this book) My beliefs were re-shaped during this stage of my life. I was *not* in control! I *don't* know the answer! *I am limited*! Oh, it was hard to go from being a leader and feeling such control to learning I wasn't in control and had to be a follower!

But, even with all this testing and shattering going on, I was still learning new skills, including a whole new level of how to communicate with others, how to be a father, how to have empathy, how to persevere, how to fail, how to manage anger, how to be flexible, how to lean on God, and many other vital skills necessary for a healthy adulthood. And I think it's important to note, I didn't just survive and learn these skills as a result—I actually *learned* these skills, which *enabled me to survive*! Now that I am on the other side of my Testing Years, I can maintain these skills and share them with others. The focus wasn't just on survival—it was on gaining new conclusions and new skills.

How about you? Have you encountered this stage? Are you in it right now? What significant events happened in your life during these Testing Years?

1. Who were the significant people in your life during your Testing Years?
2. What did you come to believe about yourself through these experiences and relationships?
3. What specific skills did you learn?
4. What beliefs did you adopt about yourself, authority, God, justice, trust, relationships? There may be many other beliefs that you're able to identify as well.

Once again: write these down! It's all part of your map!

(A side note, for your consideration...It's possible to walk through this stage and never let go of your old conclusions - to hold on to what you believe and make life, or your boss, or your spouse, or something else be the bad guy! This happens a lot. However, if you go through the Testing Years and never let go of any of your adolescent conclusions, it will cost you. You can keep your old ways of thinking, but you may lose a job, a spouse, a business, a relationship with your kid(s), or some other very precious possession. But, hey, you were successful in maintaining your conclusions and warping your environment to make them fit! One piece of evidence that you are doing this is if you keep finding yourself in the same situation again and again with your different jobs, friends, spouses, finances, and/or emotions. Have you been there? Does this make sense to you? Are you in this cycle right now? If so, it may be time to let go of some of your conclusions so you can grab hold of something new.)

The Rebuilding Years

My Rebuilding Years lasted about six years and included becoming a successful high school teacher and coach, building new friendships and renewing old ones, becoming a successful team-builder, reconciling my relationship with parents and family, nurturing a successful marriage with my incredible wife, Lisa, and becoming a leading producer at work. Much of this was due to the use of the skills I was sharpening as I grew, as well as using new skills I learned like organization and management, how to inspire, writing curriculum, mediation, classroom teaching, team-building, leadership, how to embrace struggle, goal-setting, budgeting and many more.

Almost all the stuff I felt I had lost and would never get back returned to my life—only now it felt so healthy! Some of my old shattered beliefs were replaced with a new belief that it wasn't all about me, that I was created to glorify God not myself, that God doesn't leave, that family is good, that I can be successful and healthy. My life was moving forward along a specific path and I was aware of the fruit being produced.

1. What was the next phase you moved into? How would you title it?
2. What significant events happened in your life during those years?
3. Who were the significant people in your life during those years?
4. What did you come to believe about yourself through these experiences and relationships?
5. What specific skills did you learn?
6. What beliefs did you adopt about yourself, authority, God, justice, trust, relationships? There may be many other beliefs that you're able to identify as well.

You should take the time to write all this down! It's your map!

The Expanding Years

From there, I shifted into my Expanding Years, where I learned how to be a business leader. At 37, I left the comfort of a tenured teaching position to move back to Oklahoma and become the leader of the family business (remember the one I had been fired from back when I was 25?). During my ten years in the position of Executive Director and Board Chairman of the non-profit my parents started, I learned how to be a visionary and an administrator (although I was a much better visionary!). I also learned more about leadership training and personal development. I used previously learned skills learned to inspire and teach and write curriculum for training programs and organizational structure. I had come full-circle, teaching in the same rooms where I had taught when I was 16!

These years also reshaped and expanded my belief that life is bigger than what I think, that I have a bigger purpose that I have been transformed, and that how you think—not just act—is the most important thing about you! My skills and competencies were also growing and expanding. I was learning how to run a business, how to develop and lead a board, how to mentor, business management, human resources, and program development for inner cities and global outreach.

By this point in my life, I was finally beginning to see a pattern of growth. I was recognizing my map! This recognition of my path allowed me to anticipate what was coming next; my next stage!

But how about you? How would you title your next stage? How long did it last? Are you still in it? How did the transition come about?

1. What significant events happened in your life during those years?
2. Who were the significant people in your life during those years?
3. What did you come to believe about yourself through these experiences and relationships?
4. What specific skills did you learn?
5. What beliefs did you adopt about yourself, authority, God, justice, trust, relationships? There may be many other beliefs that you're able to identify as well.

THE EXPANSION YEARS, PART TWO

Currently, I'm in my Expansion Years, Part Two. This stage started with entrepreneurialism when, at 47, I took another leap into a new arena. Because of my map of past experiences, I had the confidence to leave the comfort of a salary with benefits, a reputation with a company, and success with a product, and make the transition to starting my own company.

Today that has turned into *five* companies! Each one plays on the skills and competencies I have gained throughout my life—leadership training, life coaching, public speaking, business consulting, and a non-profit that provides programming for at-risk kids both here and overseas.

The fun thing is to know it's not the end of my journey! My map still includes more destinations! My beliefs continue to expand! I'm not done! My future isn't just more of my past! Did you get that? My future isn't just more of my past!

As you begin to develop your map, are you seeing patterns develop? Has your map revealed a course that allows you to anticipate any future destinations? Does your map reveal that you have stopped moving forward somewhere along the way? If so, can you use your map to discover what caused you to stop? What events, people or belief systems caused you to settle in to a certain spot and not go any further?

I hope you've taken the time to engage in this exercise. It's a powerful tool to help you tap into your design and your path of growth. I've had some people do this and discover that, all the way back in their twenties, they made some decisions out of fear and those decisions have set them on a course that led them away from their design. They made decisions based on security rather than destiny, but they've since decided not to be defined by their past and made a decision to chart a new course into their future!

It's not too late!

You can do this at any point of your life. You don't have to make monster changes to begin moving forward. Some people I've worked with have simply added a few activities to their lives that have allowed them to experience a major fulfillment out of their days. You can do it to! Just follow your map!

Acclaim for Clay Staires'

Programs And Personal Development Training Courses And Services
- The Forge Leadership Training
- The Eagles Nest
- The Leadership Initiative
- The Right Foundations After School Program
- The LeaderCast Training Intensive
- The Furnace Discipleship Training
- The Forerunner Discipleship Training
- Cornerstone Christian Coaching

"I was amazed that we were able to accomplish so much in just 24 hours (at *The LeaderCast Training Intensive*). I would not have believed that I would be able to witness such a change in my kids' attitude and thinking so quickly." **Mike Benson, Youth Director**

"With other experiences, they did the activities and maybe talked for one or two minutes before moving on to the next activity. At *LeaderCast Training Intensive,* we actually talked at length about what we did and how we responded. It wasn't just about the activity but about what the activity revealed!" **Owasso High School Student**

"The challenges that Clay gave us were so inviting. He lead us from one level to the next is a very personal, non-threatening way. We were excited to take the next step! The questions that Clay asked were so thought provoking and led the group into a new way of thinking. I loved *The LeaderCast Training Intensive*!" **Collinsville High School Student**

"I've not only known Clay for years, but I've been able to watch him build his leadership curriculum throughout the years as well and I truly believe it's one of the better youth leadership programs around. We all want the next generation to be more successful and fruitful than the one before it; and my hope is that leadership programs such as *The Forge* will be supported—because in my opinion—our country will be worse off without them."
Matt Pinnell, Chairman, Oklahoma State Republican Party Chairman

As a *Life Coach*, his skill level in dealing with complex issues allows him to make the hard to envision simple to achieve. My personal experience has proven that the misconceptions I had about the transition I was experiencing was brought to light by Clay, by his offering a different interpretation of my situation he opened my eyes to see the possible… where I was looking at the impossible. **Bob Townsend, Entrepreneur**

"Clay's *Coaching* style conveys ideas on a very practical, applicable level. His approach to teaching Christian leadership has been invaluable for me in my personal and professional life." **Joey Odom, Associate Director, Stan Johnson Company**

"Clay possesses both zeal and wisdom, allowing his teachings to impact you on hearing as well as for years to come. I am daily drawn closer to Jesus as I apply many of the principles that I learned under his leadership while in *The Eagles Nest*." **Martha Glover, Attorney**

"Clay's passion for the Lord and training up leaders in *The Furnace* is something special, unique and powerful. He is gifted in calling up people, calling out their gifts, training them accordingly and releasing them to bring the Kingdom to their communities." **Dana Agee, Redeemer Covenant Church**

"Through *The Furnace*, I have been equipped and empowered not only to lead, but also to equip and empower others." **Lauren Caldwell, Elementary Teacher**

Clay is one of my favorite teachers. He makes things that are boring very intriguing. Every time I walk away from one of his teachings I am excited for what is next. In *The Furnace*, he brings instruction in a way that is very applicable and easy to understand. **Claire Yinger, Bethel School of the Supernatural**

Clay Staires is the type of leader the world is looking for in its current season. His strength of character is augmented by humor, warmth, and the unyielding belief that everyone has within them the capacity to lead and better themselves. He does not fall into the trap of compassion without action, but is actively creating a road map for success for any individual, at any level. **Elliott Yinger, Land man/Entrepreneur**

"As a *Consultant*, Clay Staires has done a great job helping me to define and establish a new structured culture in our Children's Ministry. His leadership training sessions have helped our whole team gain better insight into what it means to really work as a team towards the same goal. Working with Clay has not only helped to develop the ministry but has also helped to develop me into a better leader to lead the ministry." **Candace Johnson, Children's Ministry Director**

"Clay Staires *Employee Training System* has immensely helped our team to meet our sales and growth goals. Previously to bringing in Eric (the guy that Clay trained), we had cycled through 4 new employees in an attempt to find and train a competent person who could effectively do that job. After bringing in an employee who had been trained on

Clay's system, we were able to keep the employee for over 5 years, and we grew our overall level of gross sales by nearly $300,00 per year. Clay's system delivers." – **Clay Clark - U.S. SBA Entrepreneur of the Year - Founder of DJ Connection Tulsa**

The Furnace Training System

This is the Leadership Training System Clay developed over a five-year period while employing and training hundreds of 18 to 24 year olds to turn a struggling 30-year-old brand into a sustainable, award-winning company!

Each level of this proven system is Biblically based and designed to skillfully walk leaders with "Potential" through the process of becoming leaders with "Influence" in your organization.

This training system comes with hours of professional training from Clay for your new leaders. Plus a complete video series devoted specifically to Facilitators and Mentors so you will be sure to get the very best from each session.

"Clay's curriculum of Servant Leadership is a gateway to a stimulating work environment, a jubilant marriage, and an energized perspective on all of life's twists and turns. In a world that craves independence, he teaches freedom."
Chris Goodchild, Environmental Services Supervisor & Furnace Student 2007-2011

For more information on
The Furnace Training System, visit
www.claystaires.com

NOTES

9644787R00102

Made in the USA
San Bernardino, CA
22 March 2014